Dick Horton, as a Lieutenant RNVR, was a member of the Special Forces with which this book is concerned, and prior to that was involved in the Pacific campaign as a District Officer of Guadalcanal and in the British Solomon Islands in 1942. Subsequently he served as a Lieutenant RANVR in the coastwatching section of the Royal Australian Navy and finally Lieutenant Royal Navy.

After the war he was transferred to the Malayan Civil Service and worked there during the Emergency until 1957 when he retired to live in Sussex, where he now teaches science. For his services during and after the war he was awarded the DSC, the American Silver Star and the Conspicuous Gallantry Medal of the State of Selangor, Malaya.

By the same author

The Happy Isles
Fire Over the Islands
New Georgia Pattern for Victory

D. C. HORTON

Ring of Fire

Australian Guerrilla Operations against the
Japanese in the Second World War

PANTHER
Granada Publishing

Panther Books
Granada Publishing Ltd
8 Grafton Street, London W1X 3LA

Published by Panther Books 1984

First published in Great Britain by
Leo Cooper in association with
Martin Secker and Warburg Ltd 1983

ISBN 0-586-06235-1

Printed and bound in Great Britain by
Cox & Wyman Ltd, Reading

Set in Times

To my companions in Special Forces.

'Lo! some we loved, the loveliest and best
That Time and Fate of all their Vintage prest,
*   Have drunk their Cup a Round or two before,*
And one by one crept silently to Rest.'

Contents

Illustrations

List of Maps

Introduction

This is the story of operations carried out by Special Forces behind the Japanese lines in the great arc from the Philippines to Sumatra in South-East Asia during the Second World War. Unfortunately, owing to reasons of length, it has not been possible to do other than mention briefly the work of the guerrillas in the Philippines, Malaya, the Netherlands East Indies, Dutch Borneo and Dutch New Guinea; but their work, especially in the Philippines and Malaya, was outstanding.

The narrative shows how guerrilla war in all its forms was carried out under conditions of great mental and physical stress, requiring courage of a very high order over long periods of time, rather than the hot-blooded bravery shown in battle, though on occasion it was so displayed.

The effects of guerrilla warfare, of subversive activities and sabotage in the territories the Japanese had overrun, had an enormous effect on their garrisons, who had to use much of their strength guarding their lines of communication, never knowing when and from where the next attack would come, until they were all encircled by a Ring of Fire from which there was no escape.

Acknowledgements

The author acknowledges with deep gratitude the assistance rendered by the following in making various documents, references and advice available to him:

Mr J. B. Atkinson, CBE, late Commissioner, North Borneo Armed Constabulary: the Australian War Memorial and Staff and in particular Mr P. Stanley and Mrs J. Mulqueen: Mr R. Blow DSO: Squadron Leader J. R. de Bomford RAAF: Sister W. Brands of the Dominican Sisters: Mr A. Brierley: Mr B. J. Callinan DSO, MC and William Heinemann Ltd: Mr N. Combe OBE, MC: the late Judge Maxwell Hall: Mr A. R. Muddle: the late Mr T. Harrisson DSO and the Cresset Press: the Imperial War Museum and staff: Mr Ronald McKie and Angus & Robertson Ltd: Dr C. M. Schulten: Mr A. D. Stevenson: Sir Alexander Waddell KCMG, DSC: The late Mr H. Williams: Mr W. K. Witt: Mr H. J. Wolf.

The maps and drawings are by John Mitchell.

1

The Sleeping Witch

In the faint light that comes before dawn in the tropics heavy black columns of smoke, lit by fierce orange flames and orchestrated by long rumbling explosions, began to obscure the oil tanks and houses of the storage depot near Kediri on the island of Java in the Netherlands East Indies. A confused shouting and the noise of lorries being driven hard filtered through the jungle surrounding the depot and reached two men moving fast towards the south along the bed of a small stream. Automatically they increased their pace, their camouflaged clothing, packs and Owen submachine-guns blending with the bushes and trees overhanging the stream.

The light grew stronger and they were able to make out the river which would lead them to the sea. The sounds from Kediri grew less and, after another hour, the two men, breathing hard and sweating heavily, hid themselves in the riverside bushes to rest briefly and eat some condensed rations. They had left no tracks but the blowing up of the oil tanks would have infuriated the Japanese and they knew that search parties would be out scouring the jungle in all directions for them. For Lieutenant Foster, AIF, and Sergeant Hazel, AIF, it was the fourth operation of its kind that they had carried out and, so far, the most successful.

In the secret war which went on unceasingly as the Allies drove northward through the great arc from Sumatra to the Philippines and in the Pacific, the greatest damage to the enemy was done, not by the clash of great armies and navies, but by the constant whittling away of their supplies of oil and material, the sinking of vital shipping and the cutting of the very long lines of communication which made the Japanese so vulnerable.

These tasks were carried out on an ever-increasing scale by long-range submarines, local saboteurs and by men from the Special Forces. At first the shortage of submarines and the great distances of worthwhile targets from Australia and Ceylon had made things difficult, but as the Special Forces were built up they developed their own unorthodox craft and used them very effectively. At that time, too, no suitable aircraft were available.

Two nights previously Foster and Hazel had been brought to within range of their target on Java and now, their mission completed, they were on their way to a rendezvous well within enemy waters. They knew that they would have to wait until nightfall before they could start on their difficult and dangerous journey to contact the *Mamba*, the junk-like vessel which had brought them from their base on Garden Island, south of Fremantle on the west coast of Australia; meanwhile they must endure not only the tense hours as the Japanese searched for them but also the heat and the myriad mosquitoes.

The river's banks were dense with mangroves; keeping to deep water, they made their way with agonizing slowness along its western edge, knowing that there were no villages on that side. Sometimes they could hear the Japanese calling to one another and the sight of searching sampans sent them deep into the mangroves to crouch up to their mud-plastered faces in the luke-warm water until it seemed safe to move again. Gradually they edged their way along the river. They seemed to be making for a predetermined point; several times Foster glanced around towards the jungle looking for landmarks, but the mountains rising up from the forest had patches of cloud drifting across them and he could not find what he sought.

Now they were nearing the river mouth and the estuary widened, providing a deeper band of shelter, but they could hear more voices and were thankful that the sun was beginning to go down. It was vital now to check their bearings before the short twilight of the tropics gave way to night. The clouds on the mountains were clearing, and now several jagged peaks could be seen. Then, as they waded along, two peaks came into line and they knew they were in the right position.

The tide was making and a light breeze sent rivulets slapping among the mangroves. They crouched down with their heads and guns above water and prepared to wait, only too aware of movement along the shore behind them, but able to relax a little as darkness fell and blotted out everything. Moonrise and the next stage in their getaway were two hours off.

There were lights on the water, and a burst of machine-gun fire showed that the Japanese were probing the estuary and firing at whatever seemed to move. They waited stoically, knowing that the Japanese could not see them and glad that the water was warm. Time passed, marked by the small noises of the night, the croaking of frogs, the shrilling of cicadas and the occasional harsh cry of a night-fishing heron. The water in front of them became a little lighter as the moon rose and their straining eyes peered into the shadows.

For perhaps thirty seconds the sound of increased splashing failed to attract them; then, with involuntary exclamations, they both swung round, as, with a swish and bubble of released air, the conning tower of a small submarine broke water some twenty yards out into the estuary. At once Hazel began swimming out to it, while Foster covered him, facing the shore and backing into deeper water. As Hazel reached the submarine and began unbolting the hatch cover a cloud moved away from the

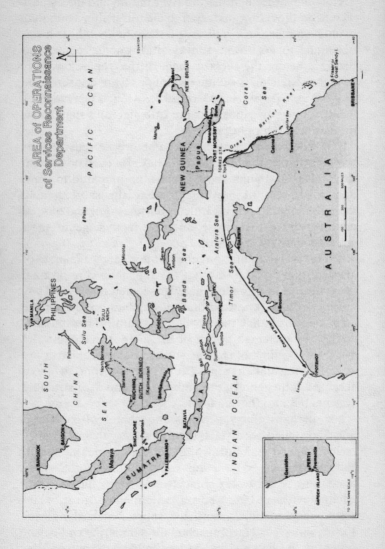

moon and its radiance lit up the estuary. A burst of rifle fire from the east bank and the chatter of a machine-gun from a sampan sent bullets splashing and whining across the water and, as Foster reached the submarine and was being hauled in by Hazel, bullets hit the submarine's casing. Hazel had the engine going as Foster clipped home the hatch, slipped the anchor cable by remote control and headed the little submarine out to sea at full speed, diving to ten feet at the same time.

The contrast to the hectic activity of the previous few minutes could not have been greater as the latest brain-child of the engineers of their peculiar organization began to prove its worth. The *Witch*, as the craft was known, was designed to carry a small group and their supplies; its unique feature being its ability to submerge and surface at preset times. For a while they could relax, as the Japanese had no way of pursuing them. Once clear of the estuary, they brought the *Witch* gently to the surface and ran awash on diesels while the batteries were recharged and their course to the south-west took them away from the shore. Hazel took over the controls and Foster attended to a graze on his left arm where a bullet had gone through his shirt. They were both very tired and tensed up but the coffee which Foster brewed and the peaceful night helped them gradually to relax. The *Witch* continued to behave impeccably as they took watch and watch about and, as dawn approached, they both stood to, ready to take the *Witch* down fast, if, as they expected, Japanese planes came out searching for them at first light. Sure enough, as the sun rose they heard the roar of aircraft to the north and at once took the *Witch* down to seventy feet where her camouflage would merge with the sea floor.

They continued on course for two hours at reduced speed; despite the arrangements for purifying the air the cramped interior of the submarine grew stifling. They risked a quick look-round at periscope depth and could see nothing, but decided to keep submerged; the risk from aircraft and patrolling ships was too great, particularly as their calculations showed that they must be very near the rendezvous with *Mamba*. They crept along on course, their anxiety rising as their frequent periscope sweeps showed nothing, until, after another hour, they sighted the silhouette of an island and emerging slowly from its shelter was a junk.

There were nets draped on her foredeck, the Japanese flag was flying and dark-skinned crewmen were busy with ropes and sail. The *Witch* approached cautiously, her pencil-thin periscope scarcely disturbing the surface until they were in the shadow between the junk and the shore when Foster brought the submarine up. At once an attap hut amidships on the junk fell flat and a Bofors cannon swung round on the *Witch*. Hazel got the hatch open in quick time, thrust his head and shoulders out and shouted,

'*Mamba* ahoy!'

At once the hail came back,

'*Witch* ahoy. Come alongside.'

The *Witch* came alongside the *Mamba* and was made fast, nestling under the high freeboard and hidden in its shadow. Excitement boiled over as Foster and Hazel scrambled aboard, filthy, smelling to high heaven and exhausted. Beers were pushed into their hands as, amid a confused babble of questions, they reported to Lieutenant Gage, the captain of the *Mamba*, that their mission had been successful and the oil tanks blown up.

There was no time to be lost in getting away and two of *Mamba's* crew went aboard the *Witch* as she was streamed astern. All the crew were multi-trained for just such an occasion and if enemy aircraft appeared the *Witch* would submerge until the danger was past. The *Mamba* turned south and was soon beating into the wind, giving the *Witch* an uncomfortable ride, so much so that her crew was changed every two hours. On the *Mamba* lookouts were doubled and, in addition to the hidden Bofors, .50 Browning machine-guns were mounted, while below decks Foster and Hazel slept the sleep of deep exhaustion, oblivious to the world. Low cloud came up and probably had the effect of preventing aircraft from Java carrying out sweeps to the south. Meanwhile the *Mamba* had turned south-east and, as the weather eased and despite her tow, she made good progress.

The day slid into afternoon and then as night fell Gage decided to break radio silence and report. Their base's call sign went out and back came the letter K. Immediately from *Mamba* went in code the words 'Mission successful' and back came the acknowledgement. The next two days saw no relaxation and then on the third day an RAAF Catalina long-range flying boat flashed them from a discreet distance for identification and they knew that they were within air cover from the fighter fields on the mainland and could ease their vigilance. Early on the fourth day the *Witch* and her tow entered Careening Bay on Garden Island and anchored off the jetty. Another operation was over.

2
Scorpion

Careening Bay on Garden Island was an ideal place for the necessarily secret operations of the seaborne arm of Special Forces and its isolation and excellent amenities could not have been more suited to the purpose. The only other inhabitants were a coastal defence battery and numerous wild creatures, among which the wallabies had the endearing habit of peering into the tents in the early morning. There were workshops and mess huts, an excellent wharf with a small crane, tents in plenty and a much valued amenity – hot showers. In view of the dangerous nature of the training there was also a resident doctor, for not all those sent to Garden Island for training could cope with the claustrophobic conditions underwater or the handling of the varied craft thought up by the backroom engineers of the parent organization.

Given names such as the *Witch*, the *Sleeping Beauty*, the *Welman*, the *Welfreighter*, these craft designed for individual type operations often developed or had inherent in them quite alarming characteristics and it required a quick hand and a controlled temperament when they misbehaved. There were also the routine training exercises involving Folboats and the use of explosives; so, inevitably, there were accidents, but fortunately no one was killed. There were other Special Force training camps scattered round Australia, such as the one north of Cairns, and another on Fraser Island off the coast near Brisbane, but the origin of all the training for subversive activities by Special Forces based in Australia, Ceylon and elsewhere was in England.

The first commando and guerrilla warfare school was at Lochailort on the west coast of Scotland and was known as the Special Training Centre. It came into being in an odd way and not because of any deep thought on the part of the War Office. A submarine carrying a party for a secret operation on the Norwegian coast had been depth-charged and so badly damaged that it had to return to Scapa Flow on the surface. The frustrated attack group then went to stay at the home of a Major Stirling in Scotland. There they thrashed out ideas for a training centre for what were to be known later as commando raids and, having received the approval of the War Office, the centre came into being.

Lieutenant-Colonel Mayfield was the commanding officer; Major Stirling was the chief instructor; Major Gavin was in charge of demolitions, and Major the Lord Lovat, a cousin of Major Stirling, came in as fieldcraft instructor and was helped by Lieutenant D. Stirling, Major Stirling's younger brother, who was later to become the originator and leader of the Special Air Service, the SAS.

The great success of the troops trained at this and other similar centres led to suggestions being made to the Australian and New Zealand governments that they might like to benefit from the British experience, and in 1940, when they accepted the idea, No 104 British Military Mission arrived in Australia to teach the new methods and expound the concept of Commando. The mission was selected from the Lochailort centre and consisted of Lieutenant-Colonel Mawhood in command; Captain (later Brigadier) Calvert RE in charge of demolitions; Captain Spencer Chapman in charge of fieldcraft; WO2 Stafford to take care of weapon training and WO2 Misselbrook to concentrate on teaching signalling.

Early in 1941, after much searching, an excellent training site was found on Wilson's Promontory, jutting out into the Tasman Sea from the extreme south point of Victoria. The Promontory, a national park, was inhabited only by a few rangers and much wild life. Its security from prying eyes was made easy by a twenty-mile isthmus of sand and scrub which joined it to the mainland. There was a tremendous variety of conditions, which made it ideal for training troops who might have to fight anywhere in the world. There were mountains, rocky crags, dense eucalyptus forests, open grasslands of all types, mud flats and scrub. There were harbours and beaches and islands and a bomber strip. The only conditions unavailable were those found in the Arctic.

The original course lasted six weeks and consisted of unarmed combat, demolition of all kinds, sabotage, living off the land, navigation by day and by night, new types of equipment, how to escape if caught, signals and weapon training and especially the use of various kinds of enemy weapons. So good was the instruction and so keen the men taking part that by the end of July, 1941, the successors to the instructors had been trained and the Australians took over the school.

Special Forces have been defined as irregular military personnel detached from regular units or specially commissioned for operations of a secret nature and their activities were given Most Secret classification. It was under this definition that, in England in 1940, there came into being the Special Operations Executive under the wing of the Ministry of Economic Warfare. First, however, it had to contend with the Intelligence Services already in being and throughout the course of the war, and after, there was no love lost between them. In 1939 there were, in England, four major Intelligence Services: the SIS (Secret Intelligence Service), also known as MI6; MI5, which was the security service; the Military Intelligence Directorate and the Naval Intelligence Division (NID). It needed the backing of the Prime Minister for SOE to get off the ground and at a later date to spread into theatres of war other than Europe and the Middle East.

In the Far East SOE spread its tentacles gradually, overcoming a shortage of supplies, complicated liaison with other governments and regular forces, difficulties with movement and training and the secure location of its own bases. Eventually from Ceylon three groups spread out. Group A operated in the Siam/Burma region; Group B, usually called Force 136, operated in the arc from the Philippines to Sumatra and the areas in between, which also took in Malaya; and Group C worked in China.

In Ceylon the Inter-Services Liaison Department (ISLD) dealt with intelligence and SOE operations. The co-ordination of their activities was carried out by Captain G. A. Garnon Williams DSO DSC RN, for it was an axiom of these operations that one group should not compromise another by knowing of its activities.

The distance between Ceylon and Australia made it urgently necessary for Force 136 to set up a base in Australia and, despite initial opposition from the Australian Government and its armed services, but with strong support from General Sir Thomas Blamey, the Australian Commander-in-Chief, in March, 1942, there was set up at 260 Domain Road, South Yarra, Melbourne, the Inter-Allied Services Department (IASD). It was headed not by a regular soldier but by a businessman who had joined up for the duration of the war. Colonel E. G. Mott had spent years in Java as a director of Maclaine Watson & Co. Ltd, which had branches all over Asia.

Colonel Mott had first been stationed in ISLD in Ceylon and when he moved to Australia he was greatly assisted by a close and unpublished working partnership

with the Director of Naval Intelligence of the Royal
Australian Navy, the brilliant Commander R. B. M. Long
OBE, and by Colonel A. G. Oldham of the Australian
Army, who had been detailed by General Blamey to join
him. Other members of the group came and went, but
the nucleus, led by Major Trappes Lomax, were from No.
101 Special Training Centre at Tanjong Balai, ten miles
west of Singapore, which had been evacuated prior to
the fall of Singapore and Malaya. There were also civilians
recruited for their special skills.

It took some time for IASD to become effective, owing
to the confused Australian/American situation following
the capture of the Philippines by the Japanese and the
subsequent flight of General MacArthur to Australia and
his assumption there of overall command. The name
suggested for the new organization was Z Special Unit, its
directive being to co-ordinate and administer a group
whose activities ranged from sabotage to the gathering of
intelligence.

On 6 July, 1942, IASD and all other Special Units came
under the control of General MacArthur and the Allied
Intelligence Bureau was formed under the direction of
Major-General Charles A. Willoughby who was General
MacArthur's Chief of Staff. The first controller of the
Bureau was an Australian, Colonel C. G. Roberts; to-
wards the end of the war he was followed by another
Australian, Colonel Kenneth Willis. The vital finances of
the Bureau were directed by Colonel Alison W. Ind, US
Army.

It was not long before Z Special had established its first
training centre in an old, unobtrusive bungalow set back
from the main road near Trinity Bay, south of Cairns in
North Queensland. Its security fence ran through clumps
of bamboo, frangipani and bougainvillea, and inside its
grounds some very mixed units went about their business,

each group keeping to itself. There were Australians, Dutchmen, Javanese, Chinese, English, Portuguese, Timorese, Torres Straits Islanders from the Cape York area of North Australia and others whose shadowy background was never revealed. It was a strange company which came and went at odd times and was known in its entirety only to the permanent staff and to those at headquarters in Melbourne.

It was from this camp that a practice raid was mounted which shattered comfortable Australian views on the security of their harbours and, until after the war, convinced many people in Townsville that they had been raided by the Japanese. Captain S. Carey, an Australian, had worked as an oil geologist in Papua/New Guinea before the war and knew the country and its people very well. He was officially on the General Staff in New Guinea compiling Topographical Intelligence, but his second occupation, unlisted and secret, was liaison officer between Z Special under the Commander-in-Chief of the New Guinea Force, Lieutenant-General Herring, and the Commander-in-Chief, Australian Forces, General Sir Thomas Blamey.

To Carey's perceptive eye a strike on shipping in Rabaul harbour on the island of New Britain would have far-reaching effects and, if his plan was approved, would only involve a few men and one submarine. In January, 1943, he proposed to General Blamey that his party, codenamed 'Scorpion', should be dropped ten miles off Rabaul harbour at night by a submarine, that they should then paddle in their Folboats into the harbour, attack the Japanese transports and cargo carriers with limpet mines and then retire to Vulcan Island (which rose inside the harbour during the 1937 eruption of the volcano, was deeply fissured and caved and was well known to Carey). There they would hide until the panic had died down and then rendezvous with the submarine. At first General Blamey told Carey that he and his party would certainly be caught and shot, but finally he agreed to the project and from then on gave it his whole-hearted backing.

Next day Carey was given a letter from General Blamey giving him over-riding priority in anything to do with his plan and he then flew south to start recruiting his party. By the end of March, 1943, he had found the men he wanted and had assembled them at the Z Special training camp outside Cairns. Four of them, Captain Cardew, Captain Gluth, Lieutenant Downey and Company Sergeant-Major Barnes, were from the 2nd/8th Battalion, AIF, and had fought in the Middle East. The others were Captain D. Macnamara, Lieutenant R. Page, Lieutenant J. Grimson, Sergeant H. Ford and Corporal G. Mackenzie. Carey, Cardew, Page and Grimson were old New Guinea hands and knew Rabaul harbour well.

Their first priority was physical fitness and the group trained hard, with emphasis on swimming, sailing and paddling the Folboats. Those who had been in New Guinea instructed the others in the topography of Rabaul harbour and all had to take a course in 'limpets' – rectangular boxes of iron each containing ten pounds of very powerful explosive known as PE (plastic explosive) which was entirely safe until detonated by a fuse. Each limpet had a strong magnet which would attach it to a steel hull; another type had a steel spike which could be stuck into a wooden hull. On one side of the box there were two holes – into one fitted the instantaneous fuse and time pencil and into the other the handling stick which was used to place the limpet some six feet below the ship's waterline; care had to be taken to prevent a clang when the powerful magnets took hold.

For maximum effect the limpets were attached in threes, linked by cordtex instantaneous fuse. The technique was for the bowman in the Folboat to attach a small magnetic holdfast to the ship's hull while his companion armed and attached the limpet; then the bowman paid out the line, a second limpet was attached further down the hull and then a third. The bowman would now detach the holdfast and the Folboat would drift away. All this had to be done in silence and in the shadow of the ship attacked. If possible, the limpets were attached at known points of weakness such as the engine room and fuel tanks.

After a final exercise, during which the group paddled 128 miles in the open sea, Carey decided that they were ready for a full-scale practice. It was 19 June, 1943, when, towards midnight, the ten men and their gear were dropped off the southbound passenger train near Black River bridge north of Townsville and south of Cairns. The Folboats were assembled and the men took to the Black River to paddle down to Halifax Bay, but the river chose not to co-operate and they spent the night and most of the next day dragging the Folboats over dry stream beds, through shallow pools and down misleading tributaries, until at dusk they reached Halifax Bay. By first light next morning they were ashore in Picnic Bay on Magnetic Island fifteen miles off Townsville.

The canoes were dismantled and carried with their stores up to Nobby Head where they made camp under cover, with no fires and a constant two-man watch. Townsville harbour, which they could see clearly through their telescope, was crowded with shipping and there were ships at anchor in the roadstead. Carey decided that four crews would attack shipping in the harbour and the fifth would limpet ships in the roadstead. It would be particularly dangerous for Carey and Mackenzie, Gluth and Page, Macnamara and Ford and Cardew and Barnes, who were to attack the harbour, as the narrow entrance and approaches were mined and there was a mine control point at the extreme end of the southern breakwater. If the Folboats were seen the watchers would assume they were Japanese and blow the mines, and the Folboats with them.

Their planning would have been better had it allowed for a moonless night; as it was when they left Picnic Bay the night was cloudless and a three-quarter moon left a phosphorescent track as the Folboats cut through the water in a broad arrowhead, but fortunately the lookouts did not see them. Towards midnight they broke pattern and Downey and Grimson altered course to attack the ships in the roadstead. The others headed for the long breakwater. Low in the water and much the same colour, they paddled and drifted slowly along the towering breakwater and slid round its end. Carey and Mackenzie were first past the mine control centre and paddled very gently into the attack, followed by the other three.

The clatter of winches, the rumble of lorries and the unloading of cargo argued that all concerned were far too busy to worry themselves over shadows on the water, so Cardew and Barnes were able to limpet two destroyers and the *Katoomba*, while Carey and Mackenzie dealt with a Dutch ship and two Liberty ships. Gluth and Page ran into a problem when they tried to attack a ship named *Akaba*: there was a barge moored alongside her and they were forced to put their limpets under the counter but in an area so small that the cord between the limpets had to be tightened and this brought them above water. However, all the Folboats managed to remain unseen and when they had planted their limpets they drifted up harbour away from the shipping to Ross Creek. Meanwhile out in the roadstead Downey and Grimson managed to put limpets on two ships but were nearly caught as they attacked a third. A deck hand lounging on the rail happened to look down, saw them and asked what they were doing.

'Just paddling around,' said Grimson nonchalantly.

'Goodnight, mate,' said the sailor.

They moved away out of his view and finished their limpeting, then paddled across the harbour following the same path as the others but keeping in the shadows all the way to Ross Creek where they contacted the others, dismantled their Folboats and had breakfast, before making tracks for Townsville and some well-earned sleep.

It was not until ten A.M. that panic broke out in the harbour, by which time, if the limpets had been armed, a number of ships would have been sunk. It began with the *Akaba* when someone pointed out that there was something strange under her counter. Soon other ships discovered similar strange objects and the Navy stopped all ship movements in the Townsville area, at the same time flashing signals to all headquarters in Australia asking for advice.

In Townsville rumours began to circulate with the speed of light – the Japanese had attacked; saboteurs had been captured; a landing was imminent. The harassed sentries and the mine control swore that nothing had passed them, while every moment ships in the harbour and the roads were expected to blow up. It was not until Colonel Ind heard the news that things began to get sorted out. He surmised that Captain Carey had something to do with the raid, and, much to his annoyance, that gentleman was woken from his sleep at 3 P.M. in Townsville and put under arrest.

Hailed before an incensed Naval authority, he explained what had happened and offered to remove the offending limpets – but ships' captains were thoroughly scared and would have nothing to do with him until he produced General Blamey's letter. The Navy, who had been trying without avail to improve the security at Townsville, were amused until they discovered that two of their destroyers had been successfully limpeted. For several days after the attack security became so tight that a fish could scarcely have swum into the harbour. Then, as on a previous occasion when the harbour at Sydney in New South Wales had been attacked by Japanese midget submarines, everything was relaxed.

The raid had been a success and showed that, if security in an Australian port was lax, it was probably as bad in Japanese-occupied ports – something which augured well for the attack of Rabaul. However, 'Scorpion' proper never took place – the Americans, who were to have carried Carey and his group, lost a submarine off Rabaul and were unwilling to provide another until the island-hopping policy initiated by General MacArthur had started, and Rabaul was by-passed and allowed to rot. For all that, the success of 'Scorpion' in Townsville harbour had a bearing on another and most remarkable operation – the longest sea raid of the Second World War, which, on the face of it, should never have been allowed but which proved one hundred per cent successful.

Colonel Mott returned to England in April, 1943, and IASD became, first, Special Operations Australia and then Services Reconnaissance Department under the command of Colonel J. Chapman Walker, another British Officer and in private life a London solicitor. At that time, when Services Reconnaissance Department badly needed a successful operation to impress on General MacArthur that it was not he and his forces alone who were fighting in the South-East Asian theatre, the Gods of War provided the means in the shape of 'Jaywick', an operation which had its origin in Malaya.

3
Jaywick

It so happened that, prior to the fall of Singapore, Captain I. Lyon of the Gordon Highlanders had been an Intelligence Officer at Army headquarters in Singapore and, when it became necessary to organize and supply an escape route across Sumatra to Ceylon and Australia, he was one of the number sent to help. The Japanese had been bombing and strafing ships and boats escaping from Singapore during the last hectic days before its surrender on 15 February, 1942, and one of the tasks allotted by the Navy to the hastily commandeered local craft was to comb the Rhio Archipelago to the south-east of Singapore, an area known as the 'thousand islands', to pick up refugees from sunken and disabled ships. Among the motley vessels operating there was an old ex-Japanese fishing boat whose name, the *Kofuku Maru*, had an immediate appeal to sailors. She was commanded by a sixty-year-old Australian named W. R. Reynolds, who had served in destroyers during the First World War; on one of his trips ferrying refugees to Sumatra Reynolds met Captain Lyon at the mouth of the Indragiri River.

Lyon, a small, wiry bundle of nervous energy, was already planning to return and attack Singapore by some means and when he saw the *Kofuku Maru* the idea of using her in some way began to form in his mind. He mentioned the idea to Reynolds and they agreed that, if they survived the present situation, they would try to meet and work out a plan based on the use of the *Kofuku Maru*. Reynolds finally managed to sail north-west up the Straits of Malacca, being machine-gunned by a 'Zero' floatplane and then rolling and pitching across the Indian Ocean, finally reaching Bombay after breaking down with engine trouble for five hours off the Nicobar Islands, their voyage a minor epic in itself.

Lyon was determined not to be caught on Sumatra and, three weeks after the fall of Singapore, he and two others, Captain J. Davis of the Malayan Police and Captain R. Broome of the Malayan Civil Service, both of whom had been involved in the escape route across Java, commandeered a big prahu, the *Sederhana Djohanis*, at Padang on Sumatra and together with Lyon's batman, Corporal T. Morris, Captain H. A. Campbell, who had been manager of a group of French rubber estates in Malaya, eleven other Europeans, a Chinaman and a Malay, set sail for Ceylon. The *Sederhana Djohanis* had no engine, her sails were rotten and she was old and unseaworthy, but there was plenty of food and water on board and, despite the fact that none of the party could navigate, there was a page torn from a school atlas which gave them a vague idea of the course to steer.

The prahu was machine-gunned by a Japanese fighter soon after leaving Sumatra and again further out in the Indian Ocean, but, apart from making her leak a little more than usual, no damage was done. The Europeans had covered themselves with bamboo matting and the Chinaman and Malay had waved, but all to no avail since the Japanese were shooting up all shipping heading away from Sumatra. After thirty-eight miserable days, during which most of them developed sores and boils, they were picked up by a freighter some 300 miles south-west of Ceylon and taken into Colombo.

The idea of a raid on Singapore continued to occupy Lyon's mind, particularly when he discovered that Reynolds had brought the *Kofuku Maru* into Bombay. He pursued his plan with single-minded ruthlessness and eventually General Wavell, then commanding in India, became interested and invoked the assistance of the Royal Navy. Lyon's plan for a raid on Singapore, using the *Kofuku Maru* (re-named the *Krait* by the Navy after the deadly Indian snake) from an Australian base, was approved. As the engine of the *Krait*, a four-cylinder Deutz diesel, had broken down, she was shipped to Sydney and arrived there aboard a British freighter in November, 1942.

Before Lyon arrived in Australia he had arranged for Captain Campbell to become the administrative head of the operation, which had been named 'Jock Force' but was changed to 'Jaywick' and put under the overall umbrella of the Services Reconnaissance Department. At first Lyon found it difficult to get active support because he had arrived at a time when priorities were being given to larger-scale operations in Papua/New Guinea and elsewhere. Added to which, the command structure under General MacArthur was unimpressed by what appeared to be a mad and apparently unimportant plan to raid the shipping in Singapore harbour. That was not surprising when the basic arrangements for Jaywick were considered – an old and unreliable ex-Japanese fishing boat with a speed of some six knots was to be sent on a voyage which might be anything up to thirteen thousand miles. There were to be one navigator (whose health, as it turned out, was suspect), one engineer, who would have to be constantly on hand throughout the voyage, and no doctor. If either the navigator or the engineer was out of action the whole operation would have to be aborted or result in disaster.

Lyon, however, was completely single-minded and his attitude was probably intensified by news that his wife and child were prisoners-of-war in Singapore. He managed to get the help of Lord Gowrie, the Governor-General of

Australia, and, through his great influence, obstacles were overcome. The approval of the Australian Naval Board was obtained and, with further backing from General Blamey and the Australian Army, Operation Jaywick began to take shape.

One of the most difficult problems in preparing Jaywick was to find a suitable crew-cum-raiding party, especially the second-in-command, for on him would fall an immense amount of responsibility. He would have to be an expert, or able to become expert, in the use of all kinds of orthodox and unorthodox arms and explosives; he must be able to train others in their use and be an expert in the handling of canoes of all kinds. It went without question that he had to be very fit and at ease under any conditions of sea and jungle.

Looking back, it could be said that from the start the crazy operation had the goodwill of the Gods, for the occasion produced the man. Lyon had been making enquiries for some days when he happened to have a meeting with an intelligence officer at Government House in Melbourne where he was the guest of Sir Winston Dugan, Governor of Victoria. As a result of this meeting he was put in contact with Lieutenant Davidson RNVR whom he had met casually once in Singapore. Davidson, an Englishman, was at that time in the Navy Office in Melbourne and frustrated.

He was physically and mentally the opposite of Ivan Lyon, being over six feet in height and big with it, quiet for much of the time but an entertaining companion when the mood took him. A physical perfectionist and a brilliant canoeist who had once canoed the full length of the Chindwin River in Burma, Davidson had been a jackeroo in Queensland and a forester in northern Siam and Burma. When war broke out he was given a commission in the Burma Frontier Force but resigned and was recommissioned into the Royal Naval Volunteer Reserve in Singapore and escaped (by small boat) via Sandakan in Borneo to rejoin his wife and child in March, 1942, in Melbourne.

Lyon and Davidson began the search for their party at Flinders Naval Depot near Melbourne where they interviewed forty men who had volunteered for 'Special Service', about which they could be told nothing. Except for two of them, the men were all about eighteen years old, had only been in the Navy for a few months and had never been to sea. Seventeen were finally selected and told that from their group only a few would be needed and that the operation for which they had volunteered was dangerous. No one withdrew.

There followed six weeks at the Army Physical and Recreational Training School at Frankston near Port Philip, where they were put through every kind of tough physical training, including unarmed combat, all under the watchful eye of Davidson. At the end of the course he selected eleven men and, early in September, 1942, the group moved to a secret training camp in a lonely spot at Broken Bay, north of Sydney.

There in Camp Z, as it was named, they went through a training schedule in comparison to which their previous experience had been child's play. For eighteen hours a day, in addition to all the commando techniques they had learnt at Wilson's Promontory Special Forces training camp, they worked at mastering the Folboats in long-distance exercises on short rations or no rations at all; they learnt to use, dismantle and put together all kinds of weapons; they became expert in the use of limpets and other explosives; for three months they had no beer, no cigarettes and no leave. They were under constant pressure, for Davidson was watching and assessing them all the time. In the long operation ahead of them it was vital that they should get along well together as they would be living cheek-by-jowl under the most difficult conditions; even one misfit might bring disaster. Finally Davidson chose five men of whom only one, Able Seaman A. M. W. Jones, had any real Navy training and sea service.

The *Krait* now came back on to the scene. Somehow its ancient Deutz diesel engine had been coaxed back to life and Reynolds brought her from Sydney and anchored off Camp Z. On 18 January, 1943, the *Krait* embarked the chosen few, together with Ivan Lyon's batman, Corporal Morris. Before he joined up Corporal Morris had been a Welsh miner, a dour man turned medical orderly in the RAMC who had earned the British Empire Medal for his work in Sumatra.

It must have caused everyone concerned much heart-ache when the *Krait*'s engine broke down off Newcastle, then again off Coffe's Harbour, before she finally staggered into Brisbane where the Navy repaired her engine. Perhaps the remote overlords in Melbourne had begun to realize, however vaguely, that the *Krait*, as she was, would never get to Singapore, let alone leave Australia, and would need constant nursing, for in Brisbane Leading Stoker P. McDowell RAN, an engineer of long experience, and Leading Seaman K. P. Cain RAN, a trained and much travelled gunner, were added to her crew before she headed north once more.

This time she managed to reach Fraser Island where she broke down, the fourth time in 600 miles. Then Davidson had an attack of malaria, something he had caught in Burma and had kept quiet about. He was taken to Maryborough hospital while the *Krait* limped northwards, stopping once more in Whitsunday Passage among the islands of the Great Barrier Reef before being towed into Townsville. It was there that Reynolds left her for another job in New Guinea and Davidson rejoined. Finally the

Krait was towed to Cairns to tie up alongside the wharf hard by Z Special Camp.

At this stage it must have taken all Lyon's insistence to persuade those concerned that Operation Jaywick was still feasible and it can only be assumed that they agreed to its continuance on the condition that the *Krait* be put into working order and be shown to be capable of several thousand miles of carefree running. Otherwise it would seem that the operation was allowed to continue simply to maintain Services Reconnaissance Department as a viable concern in the internecine warfare between the sections under General MacArthur's overall command.

The bits and pieces of the operation at last began to come together, but again there was no logical planning in the way in which the captain-cum-navigator of the *Krait* was chosen. Sub-Lieutenant Carse had been a Lieutenant in the Royal Australian Navy but had left it during the 1920s, becoming successively a school teacher, an able seaman in the Merchant Service, a third mate on a Norwegian tramp, a pearl fisher working out of Darwin, a cleaner in a Sydney factory, the owner of a camel team near Tennant Creek in the Northern Territory, a gold-digger in the Olgas, a betting-shop owner and finally an assistant in an artificial jewellery firm in Sydney.

When the Second World War broke out Carse immediately volunteered for the Royal Australian Navy but was turned down because of bronchial trouble inherited from the influenza epidemic of 1919. It was not until 1942, when the Japanese were sweeping across the Pacific, that he managed to become a Sub-Lieutenant in the Royal Australian Volunteer Reserve and was collecting small craft for harbour defence and supply in the Papua/New Guinea area when he met Commander Long in Townsville. Long had been a classmate of his and suggested that Carse could do better than wander around Papua/New

Guinea. He sent him with a letter to Colonel Mott in Melbourne and as a result Carse found himself at Z Special Camp, not knowing what was in store for him and getting bored teaching a motley collection of individuals of many races the arts of sailing, seamanship and Folboating. When the *Krait* hove into view and he was told that he would be taking her to Singapore and back he laughed loudly and told them to pull his other leg.

However, when he realized that Jaywick was serious he entered into the spirit of the raid with zest and the first thing he made clear to Lyon was that the *Krait* would need a new diesel engine and a new propeller. So Australia and Tasmania were scoured and the only available Gardner diesel engine and appurtenances were shipped to Cairns and fitted into the *Krait*. There followed for Carse and the crew the immense task of fitting out the *Krait* and storing her with such things as enough sealed food and water for at least four months, medical stores, cigarettes and tobacco, Dutch guilders to the tune of £200, all in gold for barter if it should become necessary, and separate operational supplies for the raiding parties, enough for four men for four days and known as 'Four by Fours'. Explosives included forty-five limpets and 150 lbs of Plastic Explosive. Two Lewis guns, two Bren guns, eight Sten guns, eight Owen guns, fourteen Smith and Wesson revolvers, 200 hand grenades, knives and jungle parangs and the all-important Folboats in their bags, together with single bladed, knife-edged paddles, which had proved to cause less splash and reflection and to be lighter to handle than any other types, were all stowed aboard.

Finally Carse went to Melbourne to see Commander Long and to pick up the latest information, together with the appropriate Royal Navy and Royal Dutch Navy charts. When he returned to Cairns in July, 1943, he found that the party had been rounded off by the addition of Lieutenant R. Page from the Scorpion operation, Corporal Crilley, AIF, as cook and Leading Telegraphist H. S. Young, who was to be radio operator.

Towards midnight on Monday 9 August, 1943, Carse took the *Krait* out of Cairns and set course to round Cape York and sail into the Torres Strait. Some eighteen months earlier Lyon had sailed the *Sederhana Djohanis* out of Padang carrying in his mind the idea of an attack on Singapore; it had taken all that time of searching and training before the operation was ready.

Even then the 2,400-mile journey the *Krait* was to make round the north coast of Australia to her departure point at Exmouth Gulf on the west coast of Australia was vitally necessary to prove her capabilities and to shake down her crew.

The voyage from the Pacific to the Indian Ocean took eighteen days and provided exactly what was needed to give the men confidence in the ship and in each other. It also provided some unusual incidents: when a Lewis gun was being tested an exploding cartridge caused flying glass to cut an artery on Morris's ankle and gave Page a chance to test his medical skills; they saw a whale being attacked and eaten by killer whales and Lyon revealed a strong streak of superstition, even to the extent of saying he would cancel the raid if the omens were not right. Then, one night, some instinct caused Carse to reverse course for some hours to find, when daylight came, that if they had gone ahead during the night the *Krait* would have struck uncharted reefs.

On the lighter side of things was the mistaking of the star Venus for a Japanese aircraft when they were near the Wessel Islands, bringing everyone to action stations. One practical thing that the sea taught them was that the two and a half tons of bullet-proof material laid on the deck (an idea of Lyon's based on the machine-gun attacks on the *Sederhana Djohanis*) would have to come off as the *Krait*, striking heavy seas near the Monte Bello Islands, began to bury her head and ship water.

In Exmouth Gulf the *Krait* anchored off the American Navy Base codenamed 'Potshot'. There the ship took on fresh supplies and embarked new Folboats of an improved design. These had small silk sails and were 17ft long with a beam of 2ft 6 inches, and their skins were of seven-ply rubber and canvas, which made them almost impossible to hole. The bullet-proof material was removed and Carse had the deck of the *Krait* painted grey so that, when he looked down at her from an aircraft at 3,000 ft, she was very difficult to pick out against the sea. Both Admiral Christie, who commanded the base, and Captain Hawes, in command of the submarine repair ship *Chanticleer*, found it difficult to believe that the *Krait* had come round from Cairns and doubted whether she would make Fremantle, which everyone thought was to be her next port of call. Lyon waited long enough for a telegram to arrive telling Young that he had a baby son and then, after a farewell party, the *Krait* set off and almost at once, to everyone's consternation, she stopped. The coupling key of the intermediate propeller shaft had sheared.

Captain Hawes offered immediate assistance and his engineers set to work to repair the shaft. It had to be brazed and the engineers warned that it might break down at any time. On the afternoon of 2 September, 1943, the shaft was cool and once more the *Krait* got under way with a reiterated warning from the engineers that the shaft might break down at any time. Across the mouth of the gulf there were cross-currents and a strong wind which made the *Krait* wallow and roll and made everyone except the four sailors very sick. However, by next morning the sea had gone down and the wind had slackened and when, on the second day, Carse mustered everyone late in the forenoon watch they were all alert.

Carse took the wheel while Lyon told them where they were going. The officers had known of the plan but that morning was the first time others had heard of it. Lyon told them that they were going to attack Singapore. The Japanese would not expect such an attack and, apart from sinking shipping, it would badly damage their morale and might even delay the movements of their ships into the Indian Ocean. The *Krait* would go into the Java Sea through the Lombok Strait and make for an island off Singapore from which three attacking parties would take off. There were protests from Marsh and Berryman when they realized that they would not be taking part in the attack but Lyon pointed out that one party must be kept in reserve. On the next day, he said, they would become what the *Krait* had been originally – a Japanese fishing boat. The Blue Ensign would come down and be replaced by the Japanese flag and in enemy waters there would be only one man at the wheel and one forward as was the custom of the Japanese on their fishing vessels. Everyone would stain themselves all over with a dark stain. There would be no smoking without permission and nothing was to be thrown overboard unless care was taken to sink it. No shaving mirrors were to be used in the open in case their flash gave away the *Krait*'s position. No lavatory paper was to be used; sea water would have to do. Finally, Lyon said, their mission was first and foremost sabotage and intelligence and *Krait* would do everything possible to avoid contacts, but if they were cornered they would fight.

The meteorological experts had predicted a low haze as the *Krait* moved northwards towards Nusa Besar, an island at the southern end of the Lombok Strait, but there was none and it was fortunate that the Japanese, in their overweening self-confidence, had no aircraft patrols south

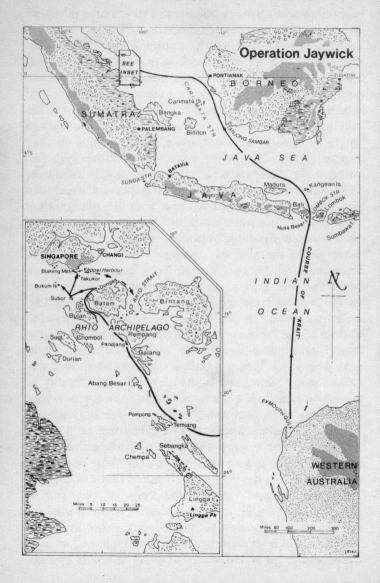

of the Indies for the sky remained a clear blue and there was no protection for the *Krait*.

Lyon's original idea had been to hide in the shadow of the 1,000 ft cliffs of Nusa Besar but Carse was against it: there was a depth of 1,200 ft at the base of the cliffs which meant that the *Krait* could not anchor and would waste fuel moving against the current and keeping men on watch. Although Nusa Besar was supposed to be uninhabited, it was only a few minutes from airstrips at Den Pasar on Bali and at Melang on Lombok. However, Lyon insisted, until the powerful current sweeping through the Straits prevented *Krait* at full power from moving forward at all and settled the argument. This was an example of poor planning, for no one had told them about the power of the current, although there was information regarding it in the Admiralty sailing directions and charts. So the *Krait* reversed course and was out of sight of land by morning.

Lyon wanted to try and get into Nusa Besar's shadow the next night but gave in when Page, Carse and Davidson all argued that the safest thing would be to approach the Strait by daylight and pass through it at night. On 8 September the *Krait* turned north once more but this time without the familiar thump of the diesel, for McDowell had fitted a silencer over the exhaust which reduced its noise to a muffled purr and cut out the glow at night. It also made sleeping easier for the men off watch.

At noon Carse spotted Gunong Agung, a peak on Bali rising from its base of dark cloud some 40 miles off, and, a little later to the east, on Lombok, the sharp outline of Gunong Rindjani cut through the clouds, at 12,000 ft the highest peak in the Indies. Their course lay right between them through the Strait. The planners had chosen the Lombok Strait in preference to the Sunda Strait, arguing that it would be less likely to be patrolled; it also gave immediate access to an enormous area of sea covered with islands among which the *Krait* could disappear.

The twenty-five-mile Lombok Strait, the Strait of the 'Red Peppers', was notorious for piracy right into the twentieth century, the pirates being mostly men from the Celebes; but now the raiders were concerned with some questions the planners had been unable to answer – was Lombok patrolled? If so would an innocent Japanese fishing boat, flying the Japanese marine flag, be allowed to pass without being challenged?

The swift tropical twilight changed day into night as the *Krait* approached the Strait for the second time and soon a full moon lifted to starboard and a searchlight blazed to the west. There was a subdued murmur of fear and excitement from the crew but they were well out of range of the light, although its reflected beam showed the angry snarls and white water of the tide rips ahead. The *Krait* lifted and curtsied as she was jostled by the savage waters and crept forward like a snail. At 8 P.M. they were almost abeam of Nusa Besar. At 10 P.M. a sight on the fixed light 1,600 ft above them on Nusa Besar to port showed that they were still only abeam of the island. By 11 P.M. they had drifted backwards a few hundred yards which meant that the current was greater than their top speed. At midnight they were again abeam of the island but for the next two hours they stayed as they were. No one could sleep.

Then at last the light on Nusa Besar showed them that the *Krait* was moving forward very slowly and by 4 A.M. Nusa Besar was six miles astern. The tide had changed. If the planners had done their job the *Krait* would have caught the north-flowing tide. As it was they were where they did not want to be, still in the middle of the Straits and right in the centre of what might be a trap. Across the Strait on the shores of Lombok they could see the tents and huts of a Japanese camp near the tree-covered village of Ampenan.

From then the *Krait* moved forward in a terrifying stillness. Everyone was afraid to speak and scarcely moved. Eyes watched the Japanese camp and each other. Slowly the *Krait* made progress until at 9 A.M. the peak of Rindjani poked through the mist and all three, Rindjani, the *Krait* and Agung, made a perfect line east to west. Bali was to port some 12 miles off and Lombok 8 miles to starboard. Carse wrote up his log at 10 A.M., some sixteen hours after entering the Straits:

Thank Christ! We are just through Lombok steering for Sekala 68 miles distant; barometer 29.9. Slightly higher. Wind SSE increasing to force 4. After clear morning, haze has now increased though Bali is still visible. Lombok is almost totally obscured.

Now they were in the Java Sea they would avoid notice as far as possible by turning away from all shipping: they would cross recognized shipping lines at right-angles and keep as much as possible to shallow water, so that, if challenged, they would keep the fight to something of their own size; lastly they would shun human contact.

The *Krait*, heading north for the Kangean group, whose scattered islands lie east of Madura, now ran into the real humid heat of landlocked water and, despite incessant buckets of salt water, it was difficult to get the temperature of the deck down sufficiently to make it bearable to the feet. As the oily scum on a sea coloured with lime green, cobalt and emerald went by, a hat and a towel went overboard and had to be retrieved. Soon after there came a welcome and unexpected relief – the ship was invaded by a swarm of butterflies which followed her and settled on her rigging. Then they were gone as suddenly as they had come.

By late afternoon the *Krait* was moving through the islands near the south-west tip of Borneo where the shallows made movement dangerous, so Carse decided to anchor. The sudden cessation of noise from the engine was a little eerie; they had been moving for two weeks without stopping and the quiet was unnerving. At first light next morning they were on their way and an hour later had passed Tanjong Sambar and turned north up the Carimata Strait. Almost at once they saw junks, one a Cantonese type and another from Batavia, both making for Borneo; a change of course soon took *Krait* clear.

All day small islands came and went and by the next dawn Pelapis was abeam to starboard and far away the mountains on Borneo showed up, while jagged against the sky to the west were the dark peaks of Carimata Island. Then, south of Pontianak, the *Krait* swung north-west and began to meet the slow swell, the dark coloured sea and the cloud-drifted sky of the China Sea.

South of Singapore the islands of the Rhio Archipelago are intersected by many narrow channels and it was thought by the planners that they would provide an excellent jumping-off place for the raid by the three Folboats. The original plan of approach meant that the *Krait* would be in narrow, shallow waters free from big ship patrols. She was to use the Temiang Strait and then cut across to the edge of the Durian Strait which separates the Rhio islands and those lying off Sumatra. The raiding parties would be dropped at Durian Island between Kundur and Sugi Islands about 35 miles south of Singapore. *Krait* would then hide in one of the Sumatran rivers where the Folboats would join her after the raid.

The nearer *Krait* got to Singapore the less the officers liked the plan and Lyon called a council of war in No 3 hold, out of hearing of the crew. It was going to be difficult to hide *Krait* in an area where people were moving about, as they would be on a river, so it was decided that she would go back and cruise off Borneo as though carrying out her normal fishing activities. Davidson was worried about the approach, the long stretch of open water between Durian Island and Singapore, and the poor getaway down Durian Strait, but Lyon ruled that first they should get to Pompong Island up the Temiang Strait.

On 15 September *Krait* was only 140 miles from Temiang and Carse was suffering from eyes so badly inflamed that he could scarcely read the sextant. He and other members of the crew had also developed watery blisters which burst and gave great pain. There was a shortage of water, for *Krait* carried only 400 gallons, and for days everyone had been on three cups of tea a day and all washing to be done in salt water. So it was with a lightening of the heart, despite a tense moment when a 10,000-ton Japanese tanker cut across their bows, that they suddenly found themselves in the midst of a violent storm known locally as a 'Sumatra'. The rain lashed down and the crew went wild; they threw off their clothes and danced and washed in the ice cold rain. For an hour they collected what water they could; then suddenly the storm was over and between the racing grey clouds a flicker of sun appeared. They were nearing Singapore and everyone knew that in a few hours they might all be dead; but, as they drank their hot tea, relaxed and refreshed, the future seemed a long way off and towards midnight, in the light of the moon, the *Krait* crossed the equator.

At dawn on 16 September *Krait* was ten miles north of the line with low cloud to the south and above that the 4,000 ft Lingga Peak in the Rhio Archipelago. Then a Japanese plane crossed between them and Sebangka Island to port. The crew went to action stations as Carse ordered half-speed but the plane continued towards Singapore, a good omen because they must have been seen and *Krait* had appeared as just another Japanese fishing boat.

Carse called for full speed and for the next five hours *Krait* was busy turning away from the canoes and fishing craft in the narrow Strait, but when they reached the heavily wooded Pompong Island its open beaches gave no protection. Another small island two miles away looked promising and they anchored off its shore but as Cain took the dinghy in to search for a break in the reef a Japanese seaplane, its yellow floats glistening, roared low across them. They waited tense, guns ready, but the plane did not return. Again their disguise had stood them in good stead. That night, making the best of a bad situation, they anchored off Pompong's eastern beach at dusk and David-son, Cain and Jones went ashore and buried emergency rations and a four-gallon drum of water. When they returned Davidson explained very carefully to the others where the cache had been made.

After dark the *Krait*'s mast was lowered to reduce her silhouette but, instead of coming down quietly, it crashed, nearly hitting Cain; their nerves were not improved when two searchlights chased across the sky to the north. Two hours before dawn they heard the roar of aircraft engines and four seaplanes streaked across the sky and then, as the light grew stronger, they heard, clear on the morning air, three words from the island in Malay. Day broke and an old grey-haired Malay in a blue sarong with two little naked boys came out of the trees carrying a small canoe. They dropped the canoe on the beach and, when they saw *Krait*, stood frozen for a second, then scuttled back into the trees.

The *Krait* moved out and away from Pompong, heading north and then north-west, searching for a raiding base until their eyes ached. Every island that looked suitable was either guarded by reefs or inhabited by people who ran when they saw the Japanese flag. All day their nerves were stretched and Carse's log speaks for them all:

September 17th 1415. Sighted OP station on Galang Baru. Increased speed. I don't know how this day is going to end . . . As long as we keep moving we do not seem to excite suspicion, but I do not think we can do it for long. We are still within about 30 miles of Singapore and still getting closer, waiting and praying for dark. No lovers longed for darkness as we do.

Lyon finally decided that Durian Island was too dangerous as a raiding base, a decision which meant that an island had to be found in the next few hours unless they were to spend another day exposed to the enemy. About 20 miles astern there had been one island, Pandjang, which looked promising, but they had kept away because of the many local fishing boats in the area. Now they decided to return to it, but in the dark; so for the time they continued along the Chombol Strait, throttled down to await the end of that nerve-racking day. Eventually the light began to fade and just before they set course for the island the clouds beyond the bows of the *Krait* began to glow a rosy red. At first Carse could not make it out, then called out excitedly, 'It's the lights of Singapore!'

As they headed in the dark down the Chombol Strait for Pandjang Island, the brilliant beam of a searchlight swept the sky ahead. It was from the Japanese Observation Post on Galang Island. Suddenly another 'Sumatra' was on them. As Carse fought the steering wheel to hold them on course a dazzling light jumped out of the darkness right ahead. As he swerved the *Krait* to starboard he recognized it as a light on one of the fishing *pagars* he had noticed on the way north. It gave him a feeling of reassurance because the *pagar* was near the mouth of the Strait. At 10 P.M. they were off the island

and able to anchor twenty yards from the shore and at 1 A.M. next morning Davidson and Jones rowed ashore. Davidson searched the jungle and hill behind the beach but could see no signs of habitation. Marsh and Berryman then began the long task of ferrying the gear ashore, freezing once in their dinghy while a Japanese patrol boat passed the island.

There was still the pick-up point to be decided and the time of rendezvous after the raid. Pandjang was too near the observation post on Galang Island, so Pompong it had to be, although it would be a long paddle. Twelve days were allowed for the raid which meant midnight on October 1st-2nd for the first pick up. The *Krait* would return forty-eight hours later if necessary. At 4 A.M. the gear was all ashore and it was time to go.

There were handshakes all round and many expressions of good luck as the crew saw them off. Then they were gone and Berryman was back with the dinghy. The anchor was up and Carse swung the ship's head towards the distant China Sea.

Daylight on Pandjang Island showed the six raiders a family of sea otters playing among the rock pools; it seemed a happy augury. On the island behind Otter Bay, as they named the place, the crew sorted and hid their supplies among the trees and tangled undergrowth. As the others worked, Davidson left to search the island. He came back in an hour to the waterhole they had found near a spring and told them that there was a small kampong (village) on the other side of the island but with no tracks coming their way.

For the next two days, with intervals for rest, they exercised to tone up their muscles, slack from almost forty days at sea. The hardest part of the journey lay ahead and they were far from fit. Early on the 20th they unpacked and began to get ready their sleek black canoes. On the attack each canoe would carry more than 6 cwt of gear, including rations for a week and survival kit. When the canoes were ready they stripped and once more dyed themselves, with emphasis on their faces and hands. Then they put on the special black two-piece suits of waterproof japara silk which were designed to grip at the wrist and ankle, two pairs of black cotton socks and black sandshoes with reinforced soles. Each man was armed with a .38 revolver and had 100 rounds of ammunition, all on a black webbing belt which could be slipped off when paddling. They carried sheath knives, compasses, first-aid kits and Lyon had with him cyanide capsules which would take effect in five seconds and which he would issue to each man before the attack.

They waited for dark and then carried the canoes down to the water. Suddenly they heard the familiar note of a Japanese patrol boat's engine. They froze as they stood in the water, confident that against the dark background they would not be seen. They had cleared the island of all trace of their occupation and in the early evening they slipped away from the island.

By midnight they had paddled about 11 miles, averaging about 2 miles an hour, and when Davidson pulled into the small, rocky, uninhabited island of Bulat they were tired and sore. They had done no canoeing for several weeks and it was an effort to unload the canoes and carry everything to a grove at the base of a cliff. Here on Bulat they learnt a lesson they were never to forget, and it was nearly the end of them. Both Davidson and Jones woke at daylight and got up immediately and looked out to sea. There, coming in slowly, was a sampan flying the Japanese flag; and they could also see two of their Folboats partly hidden by the mangroves and some supplies actually left on the beach. They kicked the others awake and then crouched in the undergrowth, their revolvers cocked, waiting tensely as the sampan anchored off the beach in full view of the bags on the sand. It stayed half an hour and then moved off.

Davidson, as the attack leader, was particularly angry with himself, but they all knew they had been equally at fault. In silence they moved everything farther into the trees and, except for the sentry on duty, spent the day sleeping. They woke in the late afternoon, very stiff and aching – and they smelt to high heaven. The special silk clothing was giving off a mixture of smells – sweat and a kind of sour milk smell which clung to them no matter how they tried to get it off. One of the few advantages of the suits was that they kept off the mosquitoes and, although the men may not have realized it, they served, unwittingly, another very useful purpose, for they concentrated all the pent-up emotions of irritation, anger, frustration, despair, fear and sheer bloody-mindedness on them. The men, living in very close contact and strung to very high levels of nervous tension, never quarrelled, worked wonderfully together and their imaginations never enlarged small and what might have been explosive incidents into anything serious.

There was no water on Bulat so they had a swim and a meal and after dusk began to paddle north along the Bulan Strait. The heavy canoes were hard enough to manage in calm water but now they were tossed about by rips and currents and at one point Lyon and Huston crashed beam on into the bow of another canoe and nearly overturned. They paddled all night, watched over by a fitful moon which shrouded itself in cloud as they carried their canoes into the mangroves on Bulan Island and hid themselves. They were very near a kampong and had to move with the greatest care as it woke to life. Dogs barked, children cried and the fisher folk passed up and down the Strait.

Slowly the sun rose, the mangrove swamp grew hotter and hotter and the sandflies, mosquitoes and small crabs became more and more active while the black glutinous mud sucked at them when they tried to sleep. Late in the afternoon heavy rain poured down, refreshing them, providing water in which to shave and to drink and making so much noise that they had to shout to be heard. When the tide turned in the early evening they left the mangroves feeling more cheerful and by midnight they were out of the Bulan Strait. Two hours later the lights of Singapore lit up the sky to the north as they reconnoitred the small island of Dongas just off the north-west coast of the bigger island of Batam, before going ashore. It was 23 September and Singapore was eight miles away. They had left Exmouth Gulf twenty-one days before and had travelled over 2,000 miles.

In the morning the party realized that they had come ashore at the only feasible landing place and that Dongas was just what they wanted, being small and uninhabited, with drinking water and a hill high enough to give a view over Singapore harbour. The effect of seeing Singapore was most marked on Lyon and Davidson, but to the others it was just another island which would involve a lot more paddling.

The telescope they carried showed ships everywhere and, leaving two sentries to watch four hours on and four hours off for signs of patrols, for signs of ships avoiding minefields and to familiarize themselves with the layout of the harbour, the rest went back downhill to their camp to make everything ready for the attack. After that they stripped themselves of their stinking clothes, hung them out to dry and tried to get some sleep between watches.

Next afternoon Lyon returned alone from his watch with Huston an hour before it ended. There were thirteen ships altogether in the roads, he told them, and it looked like a convoy getting ready to sail, an opportunity too good to be missed.

They called Huston from the lookout and climbed, grumbling, into their horrible black suits. Then they checked over their Folboats and at 8 P.M. carried them down to the water and headed for Singapore. At midnight they were still 2 miles from the roads and paddling frantically to keep the unwieldy Folboats facing the target area when suddenly a searchlight blazed over them. They froze, slumped forward, faces turned away, floating helplessly in the glare. Then the light snapped off and they began to paddle again, but at 1 A.M. Davidson whistled his thin Burma-bird call signal and they came together. The current was too strong, he said, and it would be impossible to reach their targets in time. There was nothing for it but to paddle back.

By daylight Davidson, Falls, Page and Jones were in camp on Dongas but Lyon and Huston were missing. The day wore on and their anxiety mounted. They could not sleep and prowled about aimlessly between the lookout and the camp. The afternoon was enlivened by a fierce electrical storm followed by cold rain. Then, at dusk, the missing men returned, exhausted, staggering under the weight of their limpets. They had managed to get lost on Dongas and had spent the day in a swamp.

Davidson told them that Dongas was no good with the tide as it was and that they would have to move that night and find another island to the west.

The six of them ate their rations in silence, hid their surplus supplies in a gully and carried the Folboats, operational gear and food to the beach. At dusk that night they began the long, hard paddle westwards through the tide races between the islands. Boils and blisters gave them constant pain but they drove their bodies remorselessly.

Towards dawn the small, arid island of Subor loomed up out of the mist 7 miles west of Dongas and there they landed, only to find no hiding place on the beach. Everything had to be carried to the top of the tiny rocky island and hidden among sparse bushes and stunted trees. Then they slept the sleep of utter exhaustion.

All that day the humid heat beat down on them as, 60 ft above the sea, they watched junks, prahus and sampans pass and re-pass. There was a haze lying across the face of the Singapore roads which made it impossible to see exactly where all the shipping lay; then Davidson, after an hour-long inspection through the telescope, called them together round his seawater-stained chart.

He told them that Falls and he would attack Keppel Harbour. If there were no targets they would go into the Singapore roads and attack there. Lyon and Huston would attack anything they found in the Examination Anchorage and Page and Jones would attack shipping at Bukum Island which was about 6 miles straight across from Subor.

Lyon reminded them that the rendezvous with the *Krait* was midnight on 1 October and explained that they *must* attack that night since it was already 26 September. He suggested that Davidson's Folboat, which was the fastest, should try and reach Pompong Island first to hold the *Krait* for the rest of them. It might not be necessary, but it was a wise precaution. Davidson agreed, saying that he and Falls would not go back to Dongas but would hole up along the way to Pompong Island.

Towards evening the heat lifted somewhat and their mood changed. Morale rose and they began to prepare almost eagerly for the night's action. They used the last of their canned heat to boil up billies of tea and ate a meal of meat, chocolate and vitamin pills. As the sun sank towards the horizon they heard a Japanese plane approaching and everyone fell flat, but the plane, a Japanese army transport and the only aircraft they had seen since daylight, throttled back as it prepared to land on Singapore and slid over them in the fast-gathering dusk.

They waited until the first stars appeared; then Davidson and Falls left as they had farthest to go. Fumbled handshakes in the dark and they were gone. Twenty minutes later the other two canoes were sliding silently across the dark sea under a moonless sky for the lights of Singapore.

Davidson and Falls, paddling hard, were through the passage between Tekukor and Blakang Mati soon after 9 P.M. They had a narrow escape from a big steam ferry but Davidson's keen night vision saw it moving towards them and, paddling frantically, they slid in towards the wharf and were missed by ten feet as its wash swept over them. Then they were clear and paddling up to the boom.

The boom gate was open and there was no boom defence of any kind visible as they crouched alongside. They went through the boom gate and drifted inside Keppel Harbour, where singing from the Yacht Club came clearly to their ears. Keeping in the shadows of the main wharf, they selected their first target, a heavily laden freighter, and drifted under her bows and along the side to her engine room. Falls had no trouble clamping on the holdfast and wondered why Davidson, usually so expert, was taking so long with the limpet. Then he glanced round and had the shock of his life: Davidson was calmly fixing a totally unnecessary monocle in his right eye. Falls didn't know whether to laugh or to hit Davidson over the head with his paddle. Speed was essential and here he was wasting time!

The second ship was limpeted in the same fashion but the third, a freighter with the engine aft, was so brightly lit that the reflections from the water shone on their faces like light from a fire. Then the last limpet was on, the holdfast off and the tide took them away from her side and into the darkness. All the limpets had been timed to go off at 5 A.M. but on each there was an emergency fuse giving a one-minute delay if any Folboat should be caught. The explosion would then alert the others and just give time for the Folboat to paddle out of range of the explosion.

Davidson and Falls decided to get as far away from Singapore as possible that night and, filled with exhilaration, which to some extent offset their great physical weariness, they paddled for the Rhio Strait, which, though used by more shipping, was less easy for the Japanese to patrol because it was wider. They hauled out and hid among the mangroves of Batam Island and waited. At about 5 A.M. they heard the sound of the exploding limpets and saw, far off, smoke from the burning tanker. For the rest of the day they drowsed.

Then came the roughest part of their journey, for it was now the night of 27 September and they had to get to Pompong Island by midnight on 1 October. They circled north Batam and came south through northern Rhio Strait, spending the first day on an island in the Strait and the next on Pandjang Island, narrowly missing a Japanese patrol boat. There they had their first good sleep for days, filled their water bottles and took a few packets of dry rations from the hidden supplies. Davidson left a message on a strip of paper torn from a chart. It said, 'We are proceeding to RV.'

That night they eluded the roving searchlight from the Japanese OP on Galang Island and then were nearly swamped by a 'Sumatra' which made them heave to for two hours before going ashore on an island where they spent the day in the jungle near a village. Next night they drove themselves on remorselessly and finally reached Pompong Island twenty-three hours before the RV with the *Krait*, at 1 A.M. on 1 October, more than three days after leaving their hideout on Batam Island and after thirty-three hours of paddling. They had just enough strength left to drag their canoe up under the shelter of the trees before they fell asleep. They did not wake up for fifteen hours.

* * *

The two Folboats had been paddling hard when, about 2 miles off Singapore, a searchlight swept across the water. Everyone froze, faces to decks, waiting in agony for the light to hit them. Suddenly they were full in its silvery glare. Then it danced away again and they floated in darkness. The canoes went forward. After half a mile the light leapt out of the darkness again. Again they froze. Again the light left them and again they paddled on.

Finally the treacherous currents were passed and at about 10 P.M., when they were a mile from the target area, the two teams stopped to make final preparations for their attacks. The limpets were arranged in groups of three and the fuses set for 5 A.M., plus the one-minute delay fuse. When all was ready the teams shook hands and separated.

Page and Jones turned to port and began their approach to Bukum Island where the wharf lights glittered and danced in the water. Their Folboat was soon in the glow from the reflected lights but, because anyone looking from the shore would be looking from light into darkness, the odds were that they would not be seen. Page signalled and they moved parallel to the wharves. There were welders at work on the wharf and, alongside it, on a barge. The violet-blue light from their welding arcs illuminated a large area. A freighter riding high looked a good target and, risking discovery as they crossed patches of light, they slid under her overhanging sides where it was so dark that they had to wait in order to allow their eyes to become adjusted. Then Jones clamped the small holdfast soundlessly on the side and held the cord with one hand, while pushing off the stern of the canoe with the other to give Page room to attach the limpets to the hull four feet below the water-line. Jones eased his hold again, allowing the canoe to drift backwards and enabling Page to pay out more linking fuse and attach the second limpet. The same manoeuvre was repeated down the ship's side so that the third limpet was opposite the engine room, linked to the other charges.

Jones eased off the holdfast and they paddled gently forward to hang on to the rusty anchor chain. They were eating some chocolate when some primitive sense warned them of danger and they froze. Above them, standing almost on the edge of the wharf, was a Japanese sentry with a slung rifle. He stood there for some minutes looking out to sea, then cleared his throat and spat into the water, put his rifle on his shoulder and moved off.

Page touched Jones with his paddle and they eased the canoe into the shadow of the barge. There were no other worthwhile targets nearby so they let the canoe drift outwards towards the lights of another ship to seawards. The tide was strong and Jones had difficulty with his holdfast, added to which the glare of the lights on Bukum was enough to throw a dull glow on her port side. They were about to paddle for the other side when someone on the rails threw a cigarette butt into the water. Again they froze. Then they decided to work quickly down the port side, trusting to the bulge of the overhang to protect them from view above. The ship was a modern freighter with goal-post masts and they managed, without much difficulty, to place their limpets before sliding aft with the tide, only to be caught in a cross-current which took them, before they realized it, towards another ship. They paddled hard against the tide to prevent being swept past her and at last, panting hard, managed to get hold of her rudder.

The rust was so deep on the sides of their victim, a very old, heavily loaded tramp, that it took minutes to clear a space for the limpets; but at last they were away and the lights of the tramp receded as they jettisoned their hold-fast and spare limpet and slumped exhausted in the dark. Gradually their energies revived and an immense feeling of relief swept over them. Slowly they began to paddle for Dongas Island, beginning to feel their many aches and pains but conscious of a mounting exhilaration which made it all seem worth while.

Unlike Page and Jones, Lyon and Huston had the greatest difficulty in finding a target since the total dark-ness of the anchorage and the hills behind the western end of Keppel Harbour made the approach very confusing and it was almost impossible to judge whether the lights they saw were from ships or on the shore. They searched for nearly two hours before Lyon saw a red light in the direction of Blakang Mati Island and guessed that it must be one of the tankers from Subor. They moved towards the red light and soon picked up the silhouette of the tanker against the soft glow of the city behind Blakang Mati. Slowly they circled, noting with pleasure how low in the water the ship was. Then they came under her stern. First they worked along the port side and heard voices on deck while they were putting the first set of limpets alongside the engine room. Then they moved astern to put three limpets round the propeller and were about to put the last limpet on the starboard side when Lyon felt that he was being watched and looked up. Just above him a man with his head out of a porthole was looking down at them. Huston sensed from Lyon's stillness that something was wrong and was about to whisper when the man above them sniffed. Not daring to move, they waited for a challenge. The man, who obviously had a cold, sniffed several times and cleared his throat as he slowly withdrew his head and shut the porthole.

With infinite care Lyon put on the last limpet. Huston released the holdfast and the current swept the Folboat away from the tanker. When they were out of range they turned the bow towards Dongas and gradually worked up speed, forgetting their cramps and aches as the exhilaration of having finished the job swept over them. At 4.15 A.M. they beached on Dongas, almost too tired to get out of the canoe and crawl up the beach. At 4.45 Page and Jones reached the same beach at Dongas and were so exhausted that they collapsed in the shallow water and had to drag themselves on to the sand on their hands and knees. Lyon and Huston were able to help them a little. They massaged their legs and backs and unloaded the Folboats. Then everyone was asking questions of everyone.

Page and Jones staggered unsteadily up the beach. They hid the Folboats in the undergrowth and used vines and trees to pull themselves up the hill. They had only to wait a few minutes before a thud like a distant bomb blast rolled over the water. The time was 5.15 A.M. Then came a second and much louder explosion and in the next 20 minutes they heard five more explosions. By then all the lights of Singapore and Sambo Island had gone out and ships sirens wailed across the water. They reckoned that they had sunk about 50,000 tons of shipping. (After the war it was found that No 1 Folboat had sunk the *Shinkoku Maru*, a 10,000 ton tanker. Folboat No 2 had sunk the *Hakusan Maru*, 2,197 tons, and the *Kisan Maru*, 5,077 tons, and the *Taisyo Maru*, 6,000 tons. Folboat No 3 had sunk the *Nasusan Maru*, 4,399 tons, the *Yamagat Maru*, 3,807 tons, and a third ship in the Examination Anchorage.)

Daylight brought them the spectacle of black smoke pouring from the burning tanker, also the sight of search planes and a little later the sight of many fast sampans and patrol boats. It was too dangerous to remain near the shore and they moved into the mangrove swamp, carefully obliterating any signs of their presence as they went.

Then came the awful weariness and fear of the long, long day. They lay in the filth of the swamp, fighting off the mosquitoes, listening to the drone of searching planes, panicking every time a boat passed by, listening hour after hour to the search, with the added knowledge that in the night they must paddle at least another 50 miles through dangerous and alerted waters and that they might not have the strength to reach the *Krait* – if the *Krait* had not been blown up or captured.

The worst moment came shortly before sunset when Page scrambled down from the OP to report a grey naval patrol boat passing not fifty yards from the beach and an officer in the stern examining the beach through binoculars. The patrol boat passed on and, soon after, dusk fell and they were able to come out of the swamp and prepare to move. They were still very tired, filthy from the swamp and suffering from salt-water boils, mosquito bites and hunger. However, a meal and a shave helped to submerge their despondency and fears and they all felt that things had turned out much better than they had expected.

After clearing up all traces of their occupation of the island they launched the Folboats and set out on the long paddle down Bulan Strait. It was 27 September. The currents helped them and they reached the Strait within two hours, but half a mile inside Page and Jones, who were leading, had a narrow escape when they just managed to swerve aside from an anchored Japanese patrol boat showing no lights and fortunately without a lookout. Lyon and Huston, further out in the channel, did not see the boat at all and did not stop. By midnight they were so exhausted that they landed on South Batam Island and, fortunately, without realizing it, they hid their canoes and themselves in a Chinese cemetery, a place 'tabu' to the local village and so quite safe.

They rested all day and went on that night after weathering a severe storm which nearly pushed them ashore on a rocky point outside the southern entrance to Bulan Strait. They reached Pandjang Island early on 29 September and, after finding Davidson's note, they bathed in the spring pool, ate and slept most of the day and night, intending to move on to Pompong Island on the night of 30 September, but a violent storm delayed them and as they huddled shivering under the trees Lyon decided to miss the first RV with *Krait* and go on the following night to keep the second appointment.

The dawn of 1 October came up fresh and sparkling and Lyon changed his mind. He decided to make a daylight passage to Pompong Island to make the first RV with the *Krait*. This was extremely risky but Lyon did not want to expose *Krait* to a second hazardous passage through the Temiang Strait. The others were scared of a daylight journey and distrusted his desperate decision, but they did not dispute it.

There were fifteen hours to go to the first RV when Page and Jones started for Pompong at 9 A.M. with Lyon and Huston following an hour later. At first the wind allowed them to use the small sails they had brought but when it changed they had to revert to paddling. This was their worst day. Their reserves of strength had been nearly used up, their nerves were in a bad way and their backsides were covered with rashes from their suits and friction with the canoes.

All day they paddled against the nagging south-east wind. They kept well to seaward of the islands and passed the Japanese OP off Galang without being seen. Their canoes were so low in the water that they resembled the fishing craft of the Malays and fitted into the seascape so well that float planes from the Japanese base at Chempa Island which flew over them twice during the day showed no interest. Only once, when a little too near a group of Malay fishing canoes, did heads turn to watch them. It was late in the afternoon when they pulled into a beach for a rest. They had been paddling for eight hours without stopping and they simply slumped exhausted on the damp sand, exposed to any enemy.

After an hour they drove on, suffering from the glare of the sea, their lips raw with salt, their movements mechanical, their minds a blur. On and on until at 3 A.M. on 2 October, nearly 30 miles and eighteen hours from Pandjang, they reached what they thought was the pick up anchorage on Pompong Island.

There was no *Krait*. They searched and searched, crisscrossing the anchorage until at last, worn out, they drifted into the beach, pulled the canoes up the sand and dropped exhausted.

* * *

When the *Krait* turned away after dropping the raiders on Pandjang Island on 18 September there began for her crew a period of intense anxiety, coupled with a kind of desperate boredom. She had to hide herself well away from Singapore and yet be certain that she was not seen twice in the same place among the many small islands off the Borneo coast. Carse did not dare to anchor, except at night, and so, day after day, in a state of semi-alert, *Krait* moved on an endless voyage which took her 1,500 miles while she waited for news of the raid over Japanese or other radios, and for the day when she would turn back once more to pick up the raiders. Her chances of survival were slight and her extinction would mean the almost certain end of the raiding party.

In their respective logs Carse and Young, the radio operator, kept repeating one theme – the waiting, the lack of news, direct or indirect. On 24 September Carse recorded: '*Krait*'s bottom is getting very dirty – green weed over four inches long.' On 26 September he wrote: 'Commenced scraping bottom at last . . . after wearing sarongs so long we shall probably be arrested for indecent exposure when we get back but the loose sarongs are, I think, the main reason for not getting skin disease. It seems peculiar that we should be drifting around this part of the China Sea with men working in a dinghy alongside scraping *Krait*'s bottom on a beautiful day just as if Mr Tojo had never been heard of.' On 29 September he wrote: 'Began to make back across the China Sea to keep our rendezvous. We don't know if we are walking into a trap.'

The 1st of October came and the *Krait* neared the Temiang Strait during the afternoon. It was very calm, the aftermath of the storm which had delayed them, and the evening light was so clear that Lingga Peak away to the south stood out. Dusk fell swiftly and *Krait* came to half-speed as Cain went forward to the lookout post. It would have been very difficult to see them against the brooding darkness of the China Sea but Carse was taking no chances.

Slowly, softly they moved forward, watching the fires from distant kampongs as they flickered through the night. Soon Carse ordered all guns to be manned and, as they came to the southern end of the Temiang Passage, he recognized the darker mass of Pompong Island and turned towards it. Half an hour later, at 1230, they anchored, using the heavier anchor against a strong current.

The guns, Cain with the Lewis, Crilley and Berryman with Brens and the others with Owens, covered the beach as Cain hailed once in English. There was silence. Against the faint outline of the beach a shadow seemed to be moving. Suddenly a hand slapped the gunwhale. Carse was furious. He told Davidson that he was a bloody fool not to have answered his hail and that he and Falls had nearly been shot. Davidson apologized but said he had wanted to see how well prepared they were. Carse was still angry as he listened to the noisy welcome which went on for the next ten minutes. It was endangering everything, but he realized that it was a safety valve and also how glad he was to see Davidson. But there was still the gnawing worry about the other four. Davidson and Falls took to their bunks and slept right through the pre-dawn roar of the Japanese aero-engines being warmed up on Chempa Island and at first light the *Krait* turned once more for the China Sea.

*   *   *

The noise of the aircraft engines woke Page. For a moment he did not know where he was; then memory flooded back. He was feeling sore and bruised, listening to the scratching sounds of little crabs running about in the leaves, and then, as his eyes turned past the mangroves into the Strait, there was the *Krait* a mile away and heading north. His yells and shakings woke the others and they watched silently until an island hid her from sight. Then they realized why they had missed her – they were on the wrong beach, to the west instead of to the east.

Lyon tried to console them, saying that she would be back in forty-eight hours. All that day they slept in the jungle and awoke towards evening, feeling their aches and pains but hungry for the first time for days. Lyon took some Dutch guilders from the canvas bag in his Folboat, dropped them into a pocket and went off into the trees to see whether he could contact some fishermen and get food. Page was very worried. Lyon had gone off alone and with that gold on him the fishermen, if there were any, would be just as likely to murder him as to give food. And what was there to say that they would not betray him to the Japanese, and the rest of the party?

They waited and watched in a state of increasing anxiety and restlessness but an hour before dark Lyon appeared carrying a basket filled with cooked fish and a mess of vegetables between young banana leaves. He told them that there was a camp of Malays on the other side of the island and he thought that they could be trusted.

There was smoke rising from the Malay fishing camp before dusk, so they felt emboldened to light a fire and boil some water for the last of their tea while they ate strips of cold fish and stringy bananas. Then there was nothing to do but wait. They all showed the results of days of high tension and suppressed fear; they had lost a good deal of weight and their faces were drawn, while the fading dye made their skin look even more taut than it was.

Looking across the light colour of the beach, the sea was a deep black, the sky a shade lighter. Presently it seemed to their straining eyes that a black shadow was moving. Then, 'Ship ahoy!' came the hail.

Before the echo had died away they were on their feet.

'*Krait* ahoy! *Krait* ahoy!' shouted Lyon, not caring who heard him as they dragged the Folboats down to the water, tumbled into them and dug out wildly for the *Krait*. They were alongside and engulfed in a tumultuous welcome, everyone laughing, asking questions, not listening to answers, and nobody caring about the noise until the first wild welcome was over.

Then for the first and only time in the history of the raid

Lyon called for drinks all round. Carse brought out a bottle of Beenleigh OP rum from under his bunk and Page shared it into fourteen mugs lined up on No 4 hatch. Only McDowell refused. He said that if he once started he would never stop and how would they get home? However, he did full justice to the meal when they opened up tins of reserve food and spread meat and chocolate over biscuits, eating until they were replete. Then the raiders went to their bunks. The Folboats were lifted aboard and packed into their bags and Carse turned the *Krait* away from Pompong and began the sixth and last passage of the Temiang Strait.

At 3 A.M. on 4 October they were clear and Carse set a course for the Carimata Strait across the China Sea. Luck was with them through the Madura Sea and the Kangean Islands and on 11 October at 7 A.M. Rindjani Peak was clear over the bows to the south-east. Lombok Strait and the path to safety was almost in sight. The men felt ridiculously safe, although they were still in Japanese waters and only a few minutes' flying time from Japanese-held airfields.

All day they approached the Strait without sight of ship or plane and at dark they were less than 10 miles off. At 10 P.M. they were among the tide rips and *Krait* was burying her nose in the spray. At 11 P.M. she was in the Strait, moving with the fast, south-going currents.

Then simultaneously the lookouts sighted a ship on the port quarter approaching fast. It was 11.30 P.M. and Carse turned the *Krait* towards Bali and called for action stations. He identified the ship as a Japanese destroyer of the *Sigure* class making at least 25 knots. If the *Krait* was ordered to stop and could go alongside they would fight things out, but if that was not possible they would ram her and detonate the large quantity of explosives in the hull of the *Krait*, sinking both the *Krait* and the destroyer.

About 100 yards astern and to port the destroyer slowed and turned parallel to *Krait*, then moved ahead until she was abeam, with her squat double stacks and one mast grey-white in the moonlight. She carried no steaming lights but there was a faint glow aft as from some hidden fire. Down below in the *Krait* the only noises they heard as they waited for the challenge were the muffled purr of the diesel and the slap of waves on the hull.

On deck Carse was rigid at the wheel, waiting for the searchlight challenge. Then the destroyer began to slip astern and Carse realized that her engines must have been nearly stopped and that *Krait*, helped by the current, was moving ahead. Then the destroyer moved ahead again and for eight minutes she paced the *Krait*, now less than 100 yards away. The tension was nearly intolerable. Just on midnight the destroyer increased speed and turned away across the Strait towards Lombok Island. Rigid by their guns, they saw her dwindle across the moontrack and disappear. Suddenly everybody was chattering wildly.

As the *Krait* swung round on her true course, the arguments started. Had her disguise as a Japanese fishing boat stood the test or was it because, as Carse said, the watches were just changing and the officer of the watch was tired and bored and knew that if he challenged he would lose his sleep? They would never know, but now there was a fresh upsurge of hope as the *Krait* nosed her way south. At daylight on 12 October she had cleared Lombok Strait and was beating into a strong south-easter. Next morning, when they were about 180 miles south of Lombok, Lyon decided to break radio silence and call VHM Coonawarra, near Darwin, both to report the completion of their mission and to inform Admiral Christie at Potshot base that Lombok Strait was patrolled, which would affect the approach of his submarines. Young was not too happy about breaking radio silence so close to Japanese airfields but he encoded the message and tapped out the call sign three times. There was no reply. Two days later Young tried again, this time calling VIX Fremantle and immediately received back the letter K. Young went ahead and tapped out:

To ACNB from *Krait*. Mission completed. For Admiral Christie Lombok now patrolled. ETA 17 AR.

Back came the letters RI.

Now the authorities knew that the raid had been successful and everyone could relax. Four days later, on 19 October, 1943, *Krait* anchored off the American base in Exmouth Gulf. She had headed north for Lombok forty-seven days earlier and had steamed nearly 5,000 miles. She had been in Japanese territory for thirty-three days and had struck at the heart of their dispositions without losing a single man or suffering material damage. The strain had been immense and now the raiders dispersed: some to recuperate; Lyon to Melbourne to report on 'Jaywick'; Page to Canberra to marry and Morris to Perth for medical treatment.

Carse took the *Krait* on to Darwin and handed her over to the Lugger Maintenance Section which was the cover name for Services Reconnaissance Department's base outside Darwin. Jaywick was over.

4

The Kinabalu Guerrillas

The repercussions of this remarkable and successful foray were many and at Special Force Headquarters in Melbourne there was much relief and pleasure at the complete vindication of Jaywick, for it meant that the ruling hierarchy had been shown what could be achieved by operations carried out by determined men using minimal forces.

As a result other clandestine operations under consideration were given the go-ahead and one such was to make use of the excellent material known to exist in North Borneo.

The leader of the Kinabalu guerrillas, as they were known, was Albert Kwok and he was contacted, at first indirectly, by Major F. G. Chester OBE, British Army, who, prior to the war, had been a rubber planter on Borneo's west coast and knew the area well. Force 136 put him into Borneo and he was soon *au fait* with the plans being formed by Albert Kwok and his associates, so much so that he advised them not to be impetuous but to wait until the time was ripe for an uprising. Unfortunately unforeseen circumstances precipitated the revolt, it failed and was put down by the Japanese with ruthless cruelty; but, as the narrative shows, they planted the seed of their own destruction in so doing.

Prior to the Second World War Borneo, that 'Land below the Wind', an enormous and beautiful island south of the Philippines, was divided into the states of North Borneo, Brunei, the island of Labuan, which came under control of the Straits Settlements, Sarawak and the rest of the island which was known as Dutch Borneo. The population was approximately 4,000,000, made up of the Dusuns, the Dayaks, the Muruts, the Kelabits, the Kenyahs and the Kayans, who were all people of the land, and the Bajaus, who were people of the sea. Other sections of the population were made up of Malays, Chinese, Bugis and Japanese. There were also some Indians and a few Europeans, who were either running rubber and oil palm estates or engaged in administration. Such is the nature of the country, with its few roads, rugged terrain, heavy rain forests and mountains rising steeply to the towering Mount Kinabalu at 13,455 ft that there was very little communication between the peoples inhabiting the island.

At the time of the Japanese invasion of Malaya the situation regarding the military forces was very unsatisfactory indeed, far worse than on the Malayan mainland. North Borneo had approximately 800 men under arms supported by a small force of Volunteer Auxiliaries, mainly rubber planters, for use as internment camp guards. Brunei had a small police force and Labuan an even smaller one. Sarawak had a constabulary and, before it had been formed, there had been a purely military force known as the Sarawak Rangers. As war approached they had raised a Volunteer Force and the British Government had sent a battalion, the 1/15th Punjabis, to Kuching, with a detachment of one company to the oilfield at Miri, to defend the oilfield until the planned Denial Scheme had been carried out, when they would return to Kuching, the capital.

In North Borneo extensive training was carried out and the standard of efficiency was good. In Sarawak the main purpose of the inadequate defences was to neutralize the Miri oilfields. To this end all families were evacuated and by the time war came only key men remained.

The main objective of the Japanese in their attack on North Borneo was the Miri oilfield and on Christmas Day their troops went ashore at the foot of the cliffs to the west of Miri town. As the sea was rough, owing to the northeast monsoon, they lost a number of men. Colonel Oka, a tall, thin man with a very sour expression, commanded them, and he and his men met with no opposition, since the Denial Scheme had already been carried out and the Punjabis and Royal Engineers, who carried out the demolitions, had already left for Kuching in a small ship which was subsequently attacked by a Japanese aircraft. Brunei town was quickly occupied by a column from Miri and from there the attack on Labuan and North Borneo proper was staged.

The women and children had been evacuated from Sandakan in three ships and they got through to Australia, but Jesselton was completely cut off, although the Defence Plan was put into operation and worked smoothly. However, a few days after the sinking of the *Repulse* and *Prince of Wales* off the east coast of Malaya, the War Council in Singapore ordered the North Borneo government not to resist the enemy invasion. This was done in order to save lives and, in accordance with the order, all defence posts were dismantled. On 1 January, 1942, the Japanese invaded Labuan Island by way of Mempakul, arriving at Beaufort on 3 January. Their forces were under the command of Captain Koyama and he had with him an itinerant medicine seller who turned out to be a Japanese naval officer. Another Japanese, named Sakai, who had run a photographer's shop in Jesselton, was the Civil Affairs Officer.

The Japanese reached Sandakan on the north-east coast on 13 January and there the Governor issued orders to the European officials to take no part in the Japanese administration, except in the case of the medical staff and electrical engineers. One of the first things the Japanese did was to rename the territory and divide it into two governorships. The west coast, with the interior and Kudat, was called Sekai Shiu; the east coast, with Tawau, was called Tokai Shiu. The island of Labuan was renamed Maedashima – the island of Maeda – after Marquis Maeda, the Commander-in-Chief who lost his life three months later in an air crash. Jesselton was called Api and Sandakan Elopura.

To understand what followed it has to be realized that the force behind the Japanese expansion was fundamentally their army and behind their army stood the Samurai, the Japanese ruling class. The army had built up a tremendous desire to show their strength and they over persuaded the navy, airforce and civilian government that the time had come to demonstrate Japan's overwhelming power.

Two factors finally decided the Japanese to go to war; first there was only fourteen months' supply of fuel oil left in the country and second the overriding influence of the army in the cabinet. Pearl Harbor in the Hawaiian Islands was attacked on 7 December, 1941 and between December 1941 and May 1942, the Japanese had established themselves in an arc running roughly from Akyab in Burma through the Andaman Islands along the southwest coast of Sumatra, the south coast of Java, the eastern islands of the Netherlands East Indies, the south coast of Timor, the Amboinese Islands to Dutch New Guinea then across to Salamaua on the coast of north New Guinea, then east near parallel 8'30"S and approximately 180° West, thus including New Britain, New Ireland and the northern Solomons. They named these territories the South-East Asia Co-Prosperity Sphere but not once did they allow the peoples whom they had overrun to conduct their own affairs and lead their own lives as they had done before the war under the sympathetic rule of the English, the Dutch and the Portuguese.

At first the invading force paid lip service to the Hague Convention in so far as it dealt with the treatment of prisoners-of-war and for some people this created a false sense of security.

However it was not long before the Europeans and other non-indigenous people who had been interned began to realize that the Japanese by reason of their indoctrination and beliefs were a cruel and barbarous people into whom had been instilled the view that any non-Japanese was an animal and could be treated as such.

In Borneo the Japanese demonstrated once again their total misunderstanding of how to handle people they had conquered. In their arrogance the 'Co-Prosperity Sphere' became a régime in which women were molested and conscripted as prostitutes, people were put to forced labour to increase food supplies, spies were planted in every village and food was requisitioned – initially up to 40% of the crops but, as the agents and middlemen made their profits, the total requisition rose to over 50% and led to shortages as the local farmers hid their produce – a proceeding in which they were most successful, using false partitions in the houses, the inside of mattresses or large stone jars hidden in the earth.

Perhaps the feature of their régime which the people resented most was the way in which any person, for causes however trivial, was beaten. People were slapped in public and if they showed any signs of resistance were beaten with canes or heavy wooden clubs; if further resistance was shown they were taken away to police headquarters or to prison and there beaten to death.

Another punishment was to stand the victim in the sun for hours, often with his arms outstretched. Then there was the infamous water punishment. The victim was forced to drink water until he was one large swollen carcass. The Japanese then jumped on him until water squirted out of all his orifices causing intense pain. After that most people would confess to anything – true or false.

The antipathy of the Borneo people soon turned to active hatred and this laid the foundation of guerrilla activities which, in North Borneo, reached their climax in the rising of the Double Tenth – the 10th day of October, 1943. Before that day there had been months of clandestine planning but even so the people of the country were not all united in taking an active part in guerrilla warfare. Their natures and styles of life varied considerably and it took some time for a leader to emerge and to begin the detailed liaison which led to guerrilla activities.

Of the indigenous people of North Borneo the Dusuns are farmers and have never been as warlike as the Muruts who are jungle people whose way of life involved much head-hunting. The Chinese were already at war with Japan and their position in Borneo was precarious in the extreme. They had, as a whole, supported their country's war against Japan for many years. One of the measures the Japanese took almost at once after their occupation was to confiscate all the property belonging to the Chinese and then to raise a levy of a million dollars on the west coast and four hundred thousand dollars on the east coast.

This levy led to many bankruptcies and great physical and mental distress; in addition there was a poll tax of six dollars a head. The effect of these harsh impositions was felt mostly by the Chinese; the Dusuns had most of their small savings sunk in their farms; the Muruts, being jungle people, had very little actual cash and in any case they were very hard to control. The coastal and sea people, the Bajaus, were just as hard to control as the Muruts and such wealth as they had was in their boats and fishing gear.

In a comparatively short time Japanese ineptitude, cruelty and stupidity had made the population extremely hostile to them and it was in such an atmosphere that the key figure of the first guerrilla movement in North Borneo began to carry out his work. Albert Kwok arrived in Jesselton in 1940; he had been born in Kuching where his father was a dentist; he had then been sent to Shanghai for his education and had escaped from there when the Japanese invaded the city. He managed to travel a great deal in China, visiting Nanking, Hankow and Canton among other places, studying medicine while he did so. He also joined the Red Cross and was said to have earned a commendation from General Chiang Kai-shek himself for his expertise in treating that distressing complaint known as piles and for his zeal in the interests of the Republic of China.

After a spell as an intelligence officer in the Chinese government he returned to Borneo by way of Malaya and went to live with his sister and brother-in-law in Jesselton. He was a bachelor of medium height, well groomed and strongly built. From the first he began actively to organize subversive activities and, although everyone knew he was doing this, no one betrayed him. In February, 1942, he was trying to communicate with leaders of resistance movements outside the country when he heard that there was a group of British and Dutch people on the Boelongan River. It appeared that in January, 1942, a party of twenty-one Europeans, including three women and two children, had made their way from Sibu in Sarawak to Long Nawan in Dutch territory. Four had gone on to Samarinda and eventually reached Australia. Meanwhile four Dutch airmen and others from Sarawak, some Americans and about fifty Dutch marines had made their way to Long Nawan. Albert set out to contact them with the intention of incorporating them into his guerrilla movement. He travelled alone and reached Pensiagan on the Dutch frontier 100 miles south of Jesselton but Long Nawan lay another 200 miles further south and the journey there by boat proved to be impossible because the Japanese controlled all the river craft and the arrival of a stranger would soon be noticed. So Albert had to turn back. He was never able to contact the group as they were all murdered by the Japanese in August, 1942.

It is clear from a document issued by the Japanese and dated 13 June, 1942, that *all* the Chinese in Borneo were in the gravest danger and it was not, therefore, a question of Albert Kwok placing his fellow countrymen in jeopardy by his intention to form a resistance movement. The notice read as follows:

A Warning to Oversea Chinese

The oversea Chinese have for the past five years since the China-Japan incident helped the Chungking government war-fund by subscription. The Chinese have maltreated, oppressed and denounced oversea Japanese. Such anti-Japanese conduct is intolerable. Since the outbreak of the war in East Asia, the Chinese, acting with Great Britain and the Dutch East Indies, have resisted Japan. They have behaved as an enemy, by helping the enemy. When Japanese troops repulsed Great Britain, America and the Dutch East Indies and then occupied Borneo, the Chinese changed their attitude and pretended that they knew nothing. Let not the Chinese forget that the power of seizing and putting them all to death rests with one decision of the Japanese High Command. Although the Chinese are now allowed their freedom, it is only temporary to enable the Japanese to watch their movements. Now let the Chinese reflect deeply and come to their senses before another notice.

In 1942/3 the Allied position in the area had greatly improved, especially since the Battle of the Coral Sea and the successes on the north coast of New Guinea. These victories, together with the increasing frustration and silent resistance of the people, encouraged Albert Kwok. In 1943, after an adventurous land and sea voyage, he managed to make contact with the Imam Marajukin of the Sulu Archipelago through Lim Keng Fatt, a trader in good standing, who lived in Jesselton where he was a partner in the firm of Ban Guan and Co. The firm dealt in food, liquors and household goods and was well known throughout the west coast and its staff were accustomed to meeting and dealing with foreigners.

The Imam, in peacetime, was a Moslem priest in charge of a mosque in the Sulu Islands and, apart from being a good sailor, he was well known and spoke quite reasonable English. In appearance he was short, dark and thickset and had a personality that inspired confidence. He had earlier been recruited for resistance work by the guerrillas in the Philippines and had been sent by Lieutenant-Colonel Alejandro Suarez, then commanding the 125th Infantry Regiment of the 10th Military District of the United States Forces in the Philippines, to Tawi-Tawi, an island off the east coast of Borneo and part of the Sulu Archipelago, to further the work of the guerrillas. He was disguised as a trader and it was therefore easy for Lim Keng Fatt, as a partner in a firm dealing in foodstuffs, to contact him without arousing suspicion. After their first meeting at Kuala Inanam they became firm friends.

It had seemed to Lim Keng Fatt that, as the guerrillas were holding Tawi-Tawi and neighbouring islands in the southern group, which was not far from Tambisan in North Borneo, it would be possible for them to help, particularly as the Sulu islanders had close relations with Sandakan through fealty to a common sultanate in the last century and profitable smuggling in this one. The Sulu people had never submitted to Spanish rule in the Philippines, and intermarried with them were the independent Bajaus, the sea gipsies, who were very fine sailors, brought up as they were on the unpredictable Sulu Sea, where the phenomenon of winds blowing side by side in opposite directions is not unknown, and doldrums and calms are interspersed with changing tides and sets, drifts and currents. There was, too, the sacred Bongau peak on the island of Bongau, as revered in its way as Mount Kinabalu in Borneo, for on it grows the tree of life and anyone eating its leaves will have unending life. Even more important are the four giants who live there and in times of war come down from their homes in the clouds above the peak and, hovering over the enemy, let loose violent gusts of wind and flame.

It was against this background that Lim Keng Fatt and Albert Kwok sought help from the guerrillas. On the first occasion on which Albert accompanied the Imam to Tawi-Tawi their craft was intercepted by a guerrilla patrol boat and they were hard put to it to identify themselves but once Albert met Lieutenant-Colonel Suarez, he overcame his suspicions and it was fortunate that he was able to treat and cure his Chinese wife. Soon he found himself serving with the Philippine guerrillas and was given the following identification to carry with him:

To whom it may concern: Bato Bato, 18 April, 1943
The bearer Mr Albert Kwok, of Jesselton, British North Borneo, has rendered service to the US Forces in the Philippines. He has promised to do the same in the future whenever he is needed. Consideration should be extended to him and he should not be bothered when met by any members of the Field Force.

Alejandro Suarez, Lieutenant-
Colonel, Infantry, Commanding.

He continued to give good service to the guerrillas as this letter certifies:

This is to certify that Mr Albert I. N. Kwok of Jesselton, British North Borneo, is one of my personal advisers. Sometimes I have used him in the service of the United States Army Forces in the Philippines to undertake a delicate mission.

On 11 May, 1943, Lieutenant-Colonel Suarez arranged for Albert to return to Jesselton to collect information and funds. His covering letter for the operation reads:

To whom it may concern:

The bearer Mr Albert I. N. Kwok of Jesselton, British North Borneo, has been under the service of the United States Army Force in the Philippines in the Sulu Sector. He is especially assigned by the undersigned on a mission to Jesselton, British North Borneo, as my representative on financial affairs. In as much as we are fighting side by side and fighting for the same cause, I am now appealing before you, patriotic citizens there, to extend to us your fullest co operation either by voluntary contributions or loan, and receipts will be issued and reimbursable by the United States Government of America or the Commonwealth Government of the Philippines, so that we may be able to purchase some military supplies that we badly need in order to destroy and exterminate our common enemy.

Alejandro Suarez,
Lieutenant-Colonel, Infantry,
Commanding.

Albert reached Jesselton at the end of May and stayed with Lee Khyum Fah in Lee's house at the 14th Milestone on the Tuaran road near Telipok. He quickly set about collecting funds and organizing resistance, and soon, through the active help of the Overseas Chinese Defence Association, about $11,000 had been collected and clothing and medical supplies were accumulating. Then the Japanese, through informers, discovered the plans and Albert had to hide in a remote rubber plantation while the Military Police searched the west coast for him.

In the meantime a body of patriotic and courageous Chinese met secretly at Menggatal and formed the nucleus of a guerrilla force which would co-operate with any allied force which might land at Jesselton. This was not discovered by the Japanese who continued to concentrate on Sandakan and Tawi-Tawi, allowing the guerrilla movement on the west coast to expand and to concentrate on overcoming the inertia of the people. They also arranged for the collection of money and supplies and spread news provided by Lim Keng Fatt from his clandestine receiving sets. This underground information was very successful in raising the morale of the people.

Along the east coast pockets of resistance were steadily expanding and communication with the Philippines increased. In June, 1943, Albert met the Imam on the west coast and, going back with him to Tawi-Tawi, he took clothing and medical supplies and $11,000 as a gift from the Oversea Chinese Defence Association to the guerrillas. The Japanese, meanwhile, had decided to attack the guerrillas on Tawi-Tawi and had sent off a small force, accompanied by some men from Sandakan (who were later caught and put on trial). But the Japanese had greatly underestimated the guerrillas and had to fight for three nights and days before they could disentangle themselves. When they withdrew to Sandakan they left thirty-one prisoners behind. Albert Kwok was in the area and an undated note sent to him scribbled on the back of an envelope reads as follows:

Dr Kwok—
   The Bolo battalion have captured 31 Japanese. Would you like to help us investigate them? Thanks.

Suarez.

Eventually the Bolo battalion put the captured Japanese soldiers into boats, took them out to sea, and there beheaded them and threw their bodies into the sea, in accordance with their custom.

Albert Kwok had now sufficiently impressed Lieutenant-Colonel Suarez and his followers to earn promotion to 3rd Lieutenant and to be given duty as Intelligence Officer for the west coast of North Borneo. He was no longer directing the revolt of the North Borneo people on his own but in association with the guerrillas in the Philippines.

Kwok and the Imam arrived back in Jesselton on 21 September, 1943, and found conditions on the west coast intolerable. The Imam had been entrusted with the work of obtaining intelligence, rousing the Muslim population, spreading propaganda about the success of the guerrillas in the Philippines and emphasizing the fact that United States Forces had remained in the Philippines and would presently be sending help to the people of North Borneo in the shape of arms, ammunition and men. Marajukin's standing as Imam and a Muslim made him a particularly successful agent among the non-Chinese people of the west coast. Kwok and the Imam set to work with enthusiasm to raise the morale of the people and to collect funds. Meetings were held in secret up and down the coast and not only the Chinese but the Bajaus, the Binadans and the Sulus all became involved.

Kwok was greatly assisted by Wong Tze An and a notable old man named Musah. The latter had formerly rebelled against the government and had successfully defied forces sent to catch him by hiding for three years in the jungle. He had a great reputation among the Chinese who believed that he had magical powers, much aided by a story of how on one occasion his magic gained a win for them against the Malays at football. Musah was thought to be 'kabal', i.e. invulnerable, and the Chinese put the greatest faith in him and believed in his good luck. How otherwise, they asked, could a man oppose the government for so long and then be treated as an honoured guest? Although Musah was an old man he agreed to form his own contingent at Membakut and to take action when Jesselton was attacked.

Two more Chinese, Dr Lau Lai and Cheah Loong

Ghee, were also leaders of the resistance movement. Their age, however, prevented them from taking an active role and, by keeping in the background, they remained unknown to the Japanese for a long time. Dr Lau Lai had served the government as a medical officer for many years after graduating from Hong Kong University, while Cheah Loong Ghee was a very successful merchant who had rubber estates in the Jesselton and Beaufort districts. He also had gambling, liquor and opium shops from which he had made large sums of money until they were closed down in the days of the Chartered Company. He reopened them during the Japanese occupation and once again made large profits.

The position of these two men was awkward. They handled cash and supplies for the Japanese and the guerrillas knew that if they trusted them with any of their secrets the Japanese might force them, under torture, to reveal them. One of the more difficult things they had to do was to collect a forced loan of $600,000 from the community of the west coast on the instructions of the Japanese. They had no alternative but to assess the people and make the collection which made them very unpopular, but secretly they also contributed to the guerrillas by collecting money and arms for them, though living in Jesselton under the noses of the Japanese.

One fundamental difficulty for the guerrillas was that in North Borneo there was no bond which might draw the different racial elements together and the inland tribes in particular stood aloof. For that reason Musah made a special effort to try and persuade them to join the Chinese. The Dusuns, being mostly farmers, were not by nature inclined to live dangerously, as were the Muruts, the Sulus, the Bajaus and others such as the Dayaks of Sarawak.

Albert Kwok and his friends were not alone in trying to

turn the situation to guerrilla advantage, for a section of Force 136 responsible for all Allied subversive activities on the island of Borneo was beginning to make its plans. One of the first men from Force 136 to make indirect contact with Albert Kwok was Major F. G. Chester OBE, better known as 'Gort' because of his facial resemblance to that distinguished warrior. Before the war he had been a rubber planter on the west coast and knew the area well. He began working on the east coast, paying many visits by submarine and in other ways, sometimes secretly, sometimes openly, with a cool disregard for spies and for the Japanese forces. He advised Lim Keng Fatt and his friends that the time was not yet ripe for an uprising.

This information eventually reached Mr Charles Peter, one of Kwok's right-hand men. He had been Police Chief of Jesselton before the war and was a competent and courageous man. He was in close touch with the Overseas Chinese Defence Association and through them he passed on the message to Albert Kwok. He understood the need to make haste slowly but disturbing information had reached him – the Japanese were planning to conscript 3,000 Chinese youths for forced labour and a large number of Chinese girls for prostitution. This situation was intolerable not only to Kwok but also to the other members of the Chinese community and when, in September, the Japanese began the levy – their purpose was to use the Chinese to garrison the Sulu Islands and other places where the people had beaten off the Japanese and the Japanese could not spare sufficient men to attack and garrison them in strength – Kwok decided that he must act.

He had renamed his embryo force the Kinabalu Guerrilla Defence Force (Kinabalu Mountain is regarded as sacred by a large number of the people of Borneo) and had made his headquarters at Menggatal, north-east of

Jesselton. He began to put into train the formation of more guerrilla groups at Inanam, Tuaran and Talibong and at other places along the railway, calling upon everyone to rouse themselves and to prevent further calamity falling on the community. The Japanese, with their intricate spy system, could not fail to be aware that something was afoot and made a counter move. They issued an order calling for specific men who had served in the Volunteer Force in the days of the Chartered Company to report at Jesselton police station. There the men were questioned and sounded out on their willingness to serve as a force for island garrison duty, the idea being that the Asian volunteer officers and NCOs would be in control, under Japanese officers. The implication of what was proposed soon became clear: at any moment the old volunteers who formed the nucleus of Lieutenant Kwok's guerrillas would find themselves serving in the Japanese forces.

So Kwok decided to move. He issued orders that the attack should begin on the night of Saturday, 9 October, 1943, with the aim of occupying the districts between Jesselton and Tuaran. The time selected was the eve of the 10th day of the 10th moon, commemorated in Chinese history as the day when Sun Yat-sen overthrew the Manchu dynasty on the 10th October, 1911. The Allied flag would be raised and celebration of the Double Tenth would go a long way to raise morale and attract waverers to the revolt. The force that Lieutenant Kwok had brought together was pitifully small, consisting of some 200 men from the area round Jesselton and the same number from the islands. He hoped that there would be an adequate supply of arms from the guerrillas in the Philippines and was encouraged by rumours brought in from the far-ranging fishing fleet on the east coast, but there were no firm promises and no sign of military supplies when the resolve was made to take action against the Japanese.

Lieutenant Kwok was to be in command; at Kota Belud the Deputy Assistant District Officer, Hiew Syn Yong, was in charge; Mr Charles Peter controlled the District round Tuaran; Kong Tze Phui, a former scout master, took control at Menggatal – he had already had experience of guerrilla warfare, having visited the Philippines and taken part in the Sulu War. At Tuaran there was also Subadar Dewan Singh of the Armed Constabulary to help Mr Charles Peter. Jules Stephen, formerly a sergeant of the Volunteer Force, was adjutant of the guerrillas and from the beginning was largely responsible for their organization. Meanwhile David Liew, a wireless operator in the Telecommunications Department, undertook to damage beyond repair the civilian wireless stations and a telegraph orderly, Potong by name, would remove the essential parts from the wireless equipment in All Saints Church at Jesselton.

At sea the overall command was in the hands of Orang Tua Panglima Ali of Suluk Island, and he assembled his flotilla from the surrounding islands at distant Mantanani in order to avoid raising Japanese suspicions. He was helped by Orang Tua Arshad, who led his men from Oudar Island, and two other leaders, Jemalul and Sanudin, both from the Philippines, led the Binadans of Mantanani and the Danawan Islands. The islands outside Jesselton harbour are inhabited by Bajaus, Binadans and Sulus, who were just as hostile to the Japanese as the Sulus in the Philippines, and the prospect of action roused their old piratical instincts and fighting spirits. Despite the fact that all the coastal people knew what was in prospect the secret was well kept, and, although the Japanese had spies and agents who were mostly local people, they kept quiet and the Japanese were unaware of the day fixed for the revolt. The islanders at Mantanani set out some days earlier than those living nearer the point of assembly, which was Gaya Bay, and, moving by night, used the reliable land breeze.

Although the sea Bajaus helped the Imam Marajaukin and Panglima Ali in the revolt, the land-based Bajaus would not take part, despite the fact that the Pangiran Fatimah, a princess holding land rights over a large part of the coast near Menggatal, did her full share through two of her headmen, and her home at Karambunai was always open to the Imam.

During the evening of 9 October the guerrillas armed themselves and made their way silently to their various rendezvous. Nothing stirred in the villages on the slopes of Mount Kinabalu but in the far distance a few gongs sounded as thunder rolled behind the mountain range. At 8 o'clock Lieutenant Kwok had his spearhead party ready beside the road at Menggatal. The men mounted a motor truck and it set off at full speed down the road for the small town of Tuaran with one headlight gleaming. This was the guerrilla recognition signal. The guerrillas were armed with a motley collection of weapons – some had shotguns, others carried hand grenades, some had spears and heavy clubs, there were two Thompson submachine-guns and most people had parangs. It was vital to capture more arms before attacking Jesselton. Lieutenant Kwok was in American uniform but the others wore dark clothes or just a loin cloth and smeared their bodies with soot or black paint.

The surprise of the police station at Tuaran was complete. The four Japanese soldiers and the local police were killed and six rifles and ammunition and more shotgun ammunition were taken. The guerrillas then set off for Menggatal taking with them twelve heads. At Menggatal they shot fifteen more Japanese and three more local police who had been helping the Japanese. They were all beheaded and their bodies heaped in front of the police station.

Lieutenant Kwok then selected about 100 men for the attack on Jesselton, issued what weapons he had, gave his final orders and the assault party set off for Jesselton in three trucks. But a Taiwanese had escaped the slaughter and, making his way rapidly on foot to Menggatal across the Plain of Likas, he climbed a short cut over the range at Flagstaff Hill and went down into Jesselton in time to warn the Japanese in the town. When the guerrillas arrived in the area some Japanese had already dispersed.

Nevertheless, the raiding party reached Jesselton so quickly that they caught many Japanese and leading citizens at a meeting in what was called the Koa Club and which is now the Recreation Club. The Japanese ran for the Sokyushi Club, which was on the site of the old Hylam Club at the southern end of Beach Street on the seaward side.

There were very few troops in Jesselton at the time and the land attacks and the attack from the sea were well co-ordinated and began at 10 P.M. The guerrilla trucks shot up other vehicles as they encountered them on the approach to the town. On the south road Sangyokacho Nishikawa, the chief of the Japanese prosecution department, was killed opposite the present Chinese Consulate, while Ishikawa, the police commissioner, just escaped with his life when his driver, Kassim, was shot. The guerrillas then surprised and stormed the civil police station in South Road, which contained the Japanese armoury, killing the Japanese soldiers and some military police, but sparing those local police who surrendered, including Corporal Abdul Rahman, a Malay from Singapore, who opened the armoury to them after the Japanese were dead. Later, he came under suspicion because he had not fought to the death and committed suicide by shooting himself, although the version given out by the Japanese, in order to save face, was that he had been at a

gambling farm where he had lost a great deal of money
and shot himself because he was so ashamed.

The attacks on Jesselton swept over the town from the
land by way of Likas and Flagstaff Hill and the Sulus and
other islanders climbed over the sea wall after hearing the
'sorak' (bugle) telling them to land and attack. They ran
right and left to join the land groups which had taken the
police station, killing Sergeant Kimis and P. C. Gomon by
mistake, also Mr Chin the interpreter. The results at the
police station were disappointing because the Japanese
had left only five rounds of ammunition per rifle, but at
the other end of the town they took their toll of Japanese
and lit a large bonfire on the wharf. This was in order to
attract the notice of Allied ships and submarines which, it
was thought, would come to their assistance. But, again,
that was wishful thinking and no help was forthcoming
because none had been promised or planned.

The Sulu boats, meanwhile, stood out to sea, but close
enough to hear the sorak so as to be able to move in and
take off their men. The telephone wires had been cut and
the buildings on and around the wharf were set alight with
resinous torches made of forest damar soaked in petrol.
The sheds were full of rubber and burnt for days and those
Japanese guards who retreated along the wharf were met
and killed. Another party of islanders landed near the site
of the Taiping theatre and attacked along Fraser Street,
near the market, catching and beheading any Japanese
they met. The noise of the attack and the flames rising
from the wharf were heard and seen miles away and
enabled many Japanese to take alarm and escape, but the
manager and assistant of the Nanti Co. were seen in their
car, dragged out and beheaded, and the Japanese food
controller was also caught and beheaded. Next day his
body was taken away by Japanese friends but one severed
finger lay for days on the sidewalk, a reminder to the

townsfolk of the man who had issued them with rations. Inevitably there was a good deal of indiscriminate shooting, which resulted in the death of the inoffensive Chinese driver of the town sanitary truck and his newly wedded wife as they tried to drive out of town.

The calmest man in town was Huang Tze Ann, who before the war had kept the Jesselton Stores and run the El Min press. He had converted his stores into a gambling saloon, which it had been originally, and set up an illegal lottery known as Wah Weh. He used his profits to back the guerrillas. Part of the lottery system was for the manager to publish a clue to the likely lucky number which would be drawn in the evening. That morning Huang gave 'blood on the moon' as his clue. Two officers of the Kempetai had heard it – but missed its significance.

Lieutenant Kwok kept a firm hold on his troops and there was no looting or unruly behaviour towards the civilian population. Punctually at midnight his bugles sounded and the assault parties re-formed in the market square. There, after a check on their numbers, they split up and returned to their bases in an orderly fashion. Meanwhile Kwok, using the assumed name of Wong Fah Min, issued a declaration of a state of war as commander of the North Borneo Oversea Chinese Defence Force. The declaration spelt out at length the many misdoings of the Japanese and stated that the guerrillas were prepared to fight to the end to drive the Japanese out of the country and that they had the support of the American, British and other Allied powers in fulfilling their mission.

The islanders took advantage of the night breeze as they sailed for their homes full of the excitement of the fighting which had roused their piratical blood, while the land parties, no less elated, returned to their headquarters at Menggatal, setting fire to the Inanam Bridge as they went. There was no pursuit and next morning, as the mists

cleared from the valleys, Allied flags and in particular the Chinese National flag were hoisted on all the buildings from Inanam to Tuaran for the first time since January, 1942. The Japanese thought they had destroyed them all long before.

Kwok now moved his administration to Mansiang, three miles eastward along the main road, and proceeded to mop up the Japanese remaining in the area. Ah Sang, the sub-commander of the guerrilla force, was in charge of the operations, which began with the capture of seven Japanese on the Tuaran estate. They were paraded through Tuaran and executed on 11 October.

The initial success of the guerrillas brought Kwok another 100 men, but there were still many who saw no future in the revolt and would not declare themselves for the guerrillas, while at Mansiang the guerrilla group remained inactive for three days waiting for reinforcements from the Philippines. The urgent need for arms and ammunition kept Kwok tied to the narrow strip of the coastal area under the eyes of the enemy, when he would have served the guerrilla cause better by fading into the jungle and regrouping. To some extent he was deceived by the local people, whose attitude in the first few days after the attacks was encouraging, for they had suffered greatly under the Japanese and revenge was sweet, but neither the Dusuns nor the local Muruts would help and soon the guerrillas were on the defensive.

The Imam Marajaukin had watched the beginning of the revolt and had then sailed for Tawi-Tawi to report its early success to Lim Keng Fatt and Colonel Suarez, but he did not know of the swift Japanese reaction. On 13 October they began their drive against the guerrillas. They had numbers of heavily armed troops and local police and very soon the guerrillas were driven out of Inanam and took up defensive positions between Menggatal and Talibong. The Japanese then drove towards Mansiang, using their aeroplanes and burning houses, which forced the guerrillas to move into Talibong taking their wounded with them.

The bombing increased in intensity and towns between Jesselton and Kota Belud were bombed indiscriminately, partly as a reprisal and partly to drive out the guerrillas who were forced to withdraw across the Tuaran River to its north bank. They encamped at Ranau, a small village on the banks above Temparuli Bridge. The Japanese, with their great superiority in numbers, pushed relentlessly on. They attacked and burnt the Pak Onn rubber estate buildings, in which the guerrilla rearguard under Chong Chee Syn had been holding out. He, unfortunately, was drowned while trying to swim the river to contact Lieutenant Kwok but the others withdrew in good order and joined the main group at Kampong Tambong further up the river after the Japanese had been checked at Ranau.

For the guerrillas the portents were bad. There had been no sign of help from Tawi-Tawi and it was past the middle of November. The harvest had been poor and the local people were apathetic and afraid and some of the guerrillas were anxious for the fates of their wives and children, so, to those who wished to leave, Lieutenant Kwok gave permission. He must have realized that the tide was running against him but he gave no sign of despair and his courageous bearing was exemplary even as the Japanese began to push up the valleys. Kwok had to move towards the coast to avoid being cut off and after some forced marching he and his diminished group came to the village of Kiangsam to the south. There they were able to rest for a week, but soon the Japanese heard of their presence and sent a strong force to rout them out. There followed a fierce little battle but the guerrillas could not match the Japanese strength and dispersed. Kwok and six men sought safety in the Penempang area, near Jesselton; others retired to Papar.

The seven men followed a narrow track from Kiangsam towards Penampang and arrived at the house of Liu Kai Yu near Malintud village at about one o'clock one morning. They were given shelter in a hut in the rubber estate below the house and then the son of the house went on to report contact to Chong Fu Kui, a shopkeeper at Degongan on the Penampang road, and he was able to send the small group some much-needed clothing and food while the party rested in the hut for two days and nights. During the day they climbed to the crest of the ridge above the nearby reservoir and swept the sea with binoculars and telescopes for a sight of the longed-for and promised reinforcements, but without avail. They were being helped by northern Chinese, originally from Shantung province, who, traditionally, did not get on well with southern Chinese such as Kwok, yet the common bond of hatred of the Japanese held them all together.

Across the valleys beyond the reservoir there lived the Dusuns whose headman, Majakui bin Salaman, was notorious for being very pro-Japanese. He had already tracked down and killed many of the Chinese who had left their homes during the Double Tenth uprising and it was unlikely that the presence of the seven could be hidden from him for very long, especially as there was a graded track in frequent use not far from their hideout. The danger was so great that Chong Fu Kui visited them secretly and persuaded them to move to the gravediggers' hut in the cemetery of the northern Chinese, lying between Batu Tiga and the reservoir. There, he was confident, the fear of ghosts would keep people away, and so it proved for some days, but then, through no fault of their own, they were betrayed.

Chong Fu Kui had given the man who acted as his

messenger to Lieutenant Kwok $200 to take to him, but the man, an inveterate gambler, lost the money and then returned to Chong Fu Kui to ask him to replace it. Chong Fu Kui was very angry and upbraided the man, but he brazened things out and said that unless the money was replaced he would expose everyone to the Japanese. There was a violent argument and their voices were raised. Unfortunately a spy in the pay of the Japanese was on the verandah of the shop house, listening, and as it was dark he was not seen, but he had heard enough to understand what was happening. He slipped away and reported to the headman Majakui, who in turn reported to the Japanese.

The Japanese at once ordered Majakui to produce the rebels under pain of death, but Chong Fu Kui had got to hear of what was intended and persuaded the guerrillas to move further inland and hid them in the valleys. He moved them from place to place every day and alone knew their whereabouts. Even then they could have retired deep into the mountains but at last definite news had reached them that the reinforcements from the Philippines were on their way and Kwok decided not to leave the vicinity of the coast.

Now the Japanese began to put great pressure on both Majakui and Chong Fu Kui and the end became inevitable. On 19 December at 4 A.M. over 100 Japanese soldiers set out from Batu Tiga and surrounded the area in which the guerrillas were hiding. Majakui and Chong Fu Kui were given a short time in which to produce the guerrillas, failing which they and all the inhabitants of the valley would be shot. The Japanese feared that the guerrillas would fight to the last man and, because they did not want casualties, they stayed where they were while Chong Fu Kui went forward alone; by ten o'clock he had persuaded Kwok and his men to surrender in order to save the lives of the inhabitants of the valley – or so they thought. They marched out of the hills and were taken to the Japanese officer in command, waiting for them about four miles outside Jesselton. Then the guerrillas were taken to Jesselton, handed over to the Kempetai and tortured continuously for two weeks. Kwok refused to answer any questions and tried to commit suicide; he said that he alone was responsible for the Double Tenth revolt. He was kept in Jesselton for three weeks and then sent to Batu Tiga prison.

Chong Fu Kui protested that he had done what he could for the guerrillas but his unforgiving fellow-countrymen took a different view and, as soon as Japanese protection was removed from him at the end of the war, he left Borneo and returned to China. After the war Majakui bin Salaman was tried and hanged.

Ironically the reinforcements from Tawi-Tawi under Captain Lim Keng Fatt arrived off the coast two days after Kwok and his men had surrendered. Captain Lim had with him a body of picked men, the latest types of arms and ammunition and $25,000 in cash to help the guerrillas. He soon heard of the fate that had overtaken Lieutenant Kwok and ordered a return to Tawi-Tawi, but the Japanese police learnt of his movements and pursued the islanders as far as Mantanani, in a burst of savagery massacring whole communities so that, on many islands, not a single man was left. They did this ostensibly to cut the communications between the west coast and Tawi-Tawi.

Four weeks later Captain Lim returned secretly to Jesselton in a motor-boat with four Sulus. There he picked up four Chinese guerrillas who had survived and sent them off with the Sulus to Tawi-Tawi to make arrangements to take off the remaining guerrillas while he and four Chinese companions remained ashore near the mouth of the Tuaran River.

Captain Lim, having concluded his work at Jesselton, called on the local Bajau headman, Jinal bin Arun of Srusup, to take him and his party further up the coast. The headman brought a local boat called a pakerangan to the landing stage and the party embarked. When they were nearing the mouth of the river the Bajau sitting behind Captain Lim struck him down and the boat upset. Then he and his Chinese companions were attacked in the water and killed with parangs. Next morning Captain Lim's body was seen by a Chinese on a mudbank. It was recovered and handed over to the Japanese at Tuaran and was buried on the hillside about half a mile seaward of the Tuaran District Office. After the war nemesis caught up with Jinal bin Arun and he was sentenced to death, but this was later commuted to ten years' imprisonment. The other Bajaus were sentenced to lesser terms of imprisonment. The death of Captain Lim meant that for the time being communications between the west coast and the Philippines ceased, but the guerrilla war went on, both through other Chinese and through ex-Chief Inspector Duallis of the Armed Constabulary who was a Murut.

The Muruts never collaborated with the enemy during the whole of the occupation. They were men of the jungle and, led by Duallis, they waged unceasing war against the Japanese until the Allied armies arrived. No rules were observed, no holds were barred and no trick was too mean to defeat the enemy. Duallis would brave any danger to gain a head and his ingenuity and resourcefulness were outstanding. On one occasion the Japanese sent out a reconnaissance party to march from Sapong to Rundum and Pensiagan. About thirty soldiers went and thirty Murut carriers were engaged for the journey of 120 miles, which would take about a week. Duallis saw his chance and at Kamabong secretly contacted the Murut carriers and joined the party.

One of the pleasing habits of the Muruts was to engage strangers and visitors in tests of skill and Duallis encouraged this. Whenever they stopped the Japanese were challenged to shadow boxing, single-stick fencing and other games and sports. Then the Muruts began to challenge the Japanese at running while on the march, so that, as Duallis had planned, the line of Japanese was strung out into groups of two and three. Suddenly the attack began. The Muruts were armed only with parangs and the Japanese with swords and rifles, but not a single Japanese survived.

From early in 1944 the Japanese dumps, patrols and stores on the west coast were attacked on an increasing scale, particularly by the Muruts, who had for a long time been without the stimulation of head-hunting. They continued their killings and Duallis's eventual toll was some seventy Japanese.

The final onslaught by the Muruts on the Japanese took place when the Japanese left Pensiagan to march northwards to surrender to the Australians. They were fully armed and had 200 miles to go from Pensiagan to Beaufort. No one will ever know how many Japanese were killed on the march but the fact remains that their dead and dying were spread over the whole area of the march and what was left of the total was something under 400 when they arrived at Beaufort, suffering from wounds, exhaustion and all forms of tropical disease. It was a death march for the Japanese.

Before that happened, however, the Japanese exacted a terrible revenge for the guerrilla insurrection. For six months they harried the population with search parties. One party, made up mostly of Kempetai and Japanese soldiers, searched for the guerrillas, while the other, made up of Japanese soldiers, police and local headmen, searched for the bodies of the dead Japanese. Though Musah's contingent from Membakut had not taken part in the action on Jesselton he was arrested after the uprising and sentenced to execution, but he persuaded his captors to let him off with three months' imprisonment and died in prison after serving two months.

At Tuaran many Chinese were assembled on the banks of the river, bound hand and foot, beheaded and their bodies thrown into the river. Eventually, after weeks of wanton killing, the Japanese Army administration decided to massacre their prisoners. The 21st of January was the day appointed and the place of execution was 5½ miles along the railway between Tanjong Aru and Putatan near the Patagas railway bridge. There the ground was soft and deep trenches were dug in the sandy soil. To prevent people moving through the area traffic on all roads was forbidden for three days before the execution. Those sentenced to death were mostly Chinese but the Japanese also took an appalling revenge on the islanders of the Mantanani group and the Suluk Islands near Jesselton and, further south, the Danawan and Tiga Islands. The men were either killed in front of their women and children or sent to prison, and the women and children were either imprisoned or sent to work in the ricefields. Those who were pregnant had their bellies ripped open. Very few of those imprisoned survived and none of the men – when the Allies landed on the Suluk Islands in 1945 there were only women and children left alive.

In addition to the condemned Chinese there were about a hundred Sulu men and on the 21st all the prisoners were taken to Patagas in closed railway trucks at 3 A.M. There the prisoners were lined up by the trenches and then machine-gunned, some being killed outright, others wounded and left to die a lingering death, for no one could go to their assistance.

Five leaders of the Double Tenth were selected for beheading. They were:

Albert Kwok
Charles Peter
Chan Chau Kong
Kong Tze Phui
Lee Tek Phui

The Japanese solemnly took a photograph of these men and later a copy of the photograph was found in Beaufort by the Allies. The men's heads were then struck off with a double-handed sword. In the case of Charles Peter the neck was only half-severed when he fell to the ground.

These foul crimes, instead of deterring the Chinese, aroused in them implacable hatred and hostility. Dr Lau Lai and Cheang Loong Ghee began to make secret preparations for a second revolt, while the Japanese continued with their remorseless and bloody reprisals in the name of the South-East Asia Co-Prosperity Sphere, demonstrating once again their stupidity, arrogance and inhumanity, driven on by a kind of hysterical fear peculiar to the Japanese. Funds for the second revolt were collected from all over North Borneo, with the assistance of Chinese leaders at Kudat, Sandakan and Tawau, and amounted to $250,000. All was made ready for a second revolt on 13 April, 1944.

Alas, it was an ill-omened day, for the Japanese, through their informers, had discovered what was in the wind. Both Dr Lau Lai and Cheang Loong Ghee were invited to a dinner given at the Koa Club in Jesselton on the 12th and arrested immediately afterwards. They were then subjected to the most terrible tortures. After twelve days Dr Lau Lai gave way and admitted to his complicity in the revolt, but Cheang Loong Ghee would say nothing, although strips of his own flesh were cut off and held before him. He died under torture in prison. Dr Lau Lai was hanged at Batu Tiga.

In spite of all this the Japanese were unable to put down the guerrillas. Even in Penampang there was continued fighting, especially when the rice harvest was gathered; the Japanese had to send parties of their own men to collect the rice, which were ambushed time and again by the Muruts.

Thus, in North Borneo, the spirit of resistance burned brightly from October, 1943, to October, 1945, when the last of the Japanese were rounded up and made to pay for their crimes before the Allied War Tribunals.

The Resistance in Dutch Borneo

In Dutch Borneo there had never been any real rapprochement between the Dutch and the various indigenous people. Though they had been highly organized by the Dutch with a view to commercial exploitation, this did not allow for the pride and dignity of the tribes concerned. Compared with Sarawak Dutch Borneo was better administered, but in Sarawak government organization, such as it was, took notice of the customs and wishes of the people and consequently there was a tolerance and affection for the government (before the war the house of Rajah Brooke) which was missing in the Dutch-administered territory. As a result, when the Japanese came into the area there was an uprising at Putussibau in central Borneo near the Sarawak border in which the local people murdered the Dutch administrator.

Lieutenant Davijd, of the Royal Netherlands East Indies Army, was then at Sintang on the Kaupas River in West Borneo and went to Putussibau to sort things out. This he did and, on returning to Sintang, heard that other troops there had capitulated to the Japanese. He refused to do so and formed a guerrilla group, getting away with three European Non-Commissioned Officers and a civilian on the night of 16 March, 1942, to Putussibau where he held out for three months under very difficult circumstances. At the end of June the Japanese sent 200 troops against the little force and Davijd was forced to go on the run, taking with him another seven men and two women, intending to reach the east coast, about 270 miles away across a high mountain range. After a most arduous journey they reached the sources of the Mahakam River and there they heard that Samarinda had already been taken by the Japanese.

The Dayaks on the upper reaches of the Mahakam were very frightened of the Japanese and Lieutenant Davijd had to move his small group back to the upper reaches of the Kaupas River. There they settled, but in October, 1942, the Punan Dayaks attacked them, killing all the men and bringing the two women and the bodies of the men to the Japanese at Putussibau. Here the murdered men were buried with full military honours, another example of the unpredictability of the Japanese. So ended the last attempt by the Dutch to carry out guerrilla operations in Dutch Borneo.

5

Agas and Semut

Meanwhile Special Operations Executive, in the guise of the Services Reconnaissance Department, had become very much the mother organization of all the non-American Allied guerrilla and subversive operations in the Far East. But it was not easy to find people who knew from past experience anything about the territories in which Force 136 wished to operate and who had not already been compromised in some way. Such people also had to have the necessary qualities of fitness and the ability to operate alone in dangerous circumstances. The situation led to much delving and burrowing by Special Operations Executive in London where Colonel Egerton Mott had become one of the *dei ex machina* responsible for choosing men to operate in Force 136's Far Eastern domain.

Those who volunteered (all Force 136 men and women were volunteers and could withdraw or be removed at any time with no questions asked on either side) were tested in various complicated lethal ways in Scotland, and after surviving the hurly-burly of parachuting at Ringway and passing through many odd experiences in stately homes up and down the English countryside, if not found wanting, were thereafter dispatched with top priority to their operational areas in so much secrecy that Services Reconnaissance Department and its satellite stations often did not know who was coming to them or when.

When Colonel Mott was charged with finding people who could start subversive operations in Borneo of the kind which had proved so successful in Malaya under the auspices of Messrs Spencer Chapman, Broome, Davis and others of Force 136 he turned to MI5 in London who sifted through their files and came up with one Tom Harrisson.

Harrisson had already achieved considerable notoriety by his somewhat unorthodox feats both at Oxford and Cambridge. He had also taken part in expeditions to the New Hebrides, Sarawak and the Arctic, to say nothing of his studies with Charles Madge and others into what was known as Mass Observation. He had not fitted well into the conventional army and had reached the imposing rank of Second-Lieutenant in the Green Howards Armoured Car Regiment, his views and extra-territorial activities having made him an object of scorn and loathing to his very regular Colonel.

When, therefore, Egerton Mott offered him the prospect of returning to Sarawak, a country of which he was fond, in a highly secret unit in which his independence of mind and his soaring ego would be given full outlet, he accepted at once. There were two other factors which influenced him – he had a deep-seated desire to justify himself to his father, who had taken a poor view of his activities to date, and in the forthcoming action he hoped to emerge with credit and possibly with a suitable decoration; secondly, he had been described in scathing terms by the Curator of the Sarawak Museum, Mr E. Banks, when he had visited Sarawak with the Oxford University expedition as an ornithologist. Again he felt the need to justify himself. It was just as well that he had no foreknowledge of an episode which was to take place after the war when he met Egerton Mott once again. Mott had by then become an important official in the Colonial Development Corporation and told Harrisson that he had been selected by mistake. MI5 had meant to send Mott a Harrison, well known for his left-wing views and for his efforts in the Spanish Civil War, which had given him some knowledge of cloak-and-dagger tactics. Just a matter of a small spelling mistake.

However, in Harrisson's case, celestial arrangements were, as usual, completely justified – and seen to be so. He passed the next few weeks in concentrated training, which suited his temperament and gave him confidence in his ability to survive in whatever situation might present itself. He found, also, that the independence which Force 136 expected of its executives was much to his liking and stood him in good stead when he arrived in Perth, Western Australia, via Catalina flying boat, the only aircraft then able to fly the long distance from Colombo to Perth.

No one had expected him, nor did he know where to go, so the first few days were spent getting used to, and recovering from, Australian hospitality. He was then put on a freight plane to Melbourne where he spent a delight-ful week enjoying the hospitality of the Military Club and explaining to the assembled soldiery how to drink Pernod. In due course he discovered the whereabouts of the Services Reconnaissance Department where his appear-ance came as something of a surprise. No one had signalled his impending arrival.

However, he was soon taken in hand and sent first, with Major R. G. P. N. Combe, who had been a senior administrator in North Borneo before the war, to a Special Commando School on Great Sandy Island at the south end of the Great Barrier Reef. They soon found that they had nothing to learn from the training, but Harrisson was able to brush up his Malay on the insistence of Major Combe with whom he shared a tent and who made him speak Malay at all times.

Combe was to take part in the North Borneo operation codenamed 'Agas' (Sandfly) and Harrisson was to mount the Sarawak operation codenamed 'Semut' (Ant). In accordance with procedure, there was to be no operational or intelligence contact between the Sandflies and the Ants.

Agas

In the first week of February, 1945, the submarine USS *Tuna* sailed from Darwin to land Agas, in the shape of Major Chester, British Army, Major R. G. P. N. Combe, British Army, Lieutenant F.Olsen, AIF, Staff-Sergeant G.Greenwood, NZ Forces, Staff-Sergeant V. Sharpe, NZ Forces, Sergeant Wong Sue, RAAF, and Corporal Kanun bin Garfu, AIF, on the west coast of North Borneo. A reconnaissance of the proposed insertion point located an enemy radar station which made it impossible to land the party and they were returned, via a night rendezvous, to Fremantle on the USS *Bream*.

A second attempt, using the USS *Tuna*, landed the party between two strongly held enemy posts at Tagabang and Puru Puru Island on the east coast of North Borneo on 3 March, 1945. This time the party consisted of Major Chester, Captain Sutcliffe, British Army, Lieutenant Olsen, AIF, Staff-Sergeant Greenwood, Sergeant Wong Sue and Corporal Hywood, AIF.

The party established itself some miles inland and made radio contact with Headquarters which was then in Melbourne. The mission was to establish a base, set up an intelligence network, conduct subversive activities and obtain detailed information of the prisoner-of-war camp at Sandakan in which there were some 2,400 Allied servicemen of whom nothing had been heard. Quickly the party contacted pro-Allied local people and, to encourage them further, the insertion of Agas II by parachute was made on 3 May, 1945. The party comprised Major R. G. P. N. Combe, Captain D. May, Sergeant J. Watts and Corporal Maaruff bin Ali, AIF.

Agas I and II operated successfully under the noses of the Japanese and established a comprehensive network of agents and trained guerrillas, who obtained valuable information about the dispositions of the Japanese and ambushed outlying Japanese posts and troops on the move. The further operations of the two groups concerned the removal of the prisoners-of-war from Sandakan to Ranau 165 miles away and South-West Pacific Area Headquarters' intelligence requirements for the proposed full-scale landing of Australian troops in the Brunei Bay area of the west coast.

On 20 May, 1945, Major Chester handed over command of Agas to Captain Sutcliffe; he and Sergeant Wong Sue, Corporal Hywood and one of the local people were taken by Catalina to Morotai where they were refitted and flown to the headquarters of the US Airforce group at Palawan. Then, during the evening of 29 May, the party was landed at Kimanis Bay north of Labuan Island by Catalina and remained in the area until 9 June, relaying information on all aspects of enemy organization.

On 21 June, 1945, Agas III, in the shape of Flight-Lieutenant G. Ripley and Sergeant A. Hywood, made their way under extreme difficulties to Ranau to attempt to rescue some prisoners-of-war. They found, on arrival, that there were a few prisoners all in a very weakened state, and that it would be quite impossible to bring them out. Later information revealed that of the original 2,400 prisoners in Sandakan, only *six* survived the terrible Borneo death march. Agas III, its task done, was extracted on 11 October, 1945.

Agas IV was commanded by Major R. Blow, an Australian who had been a District Officer in North Borneo before the war and had been interned in the prison camp at Sandakan. He had escaped during the march from Sandakan to Ranau and had reached the southern Philippines.

There he operated as a highly successful guerrilla leader, earning himself the Distinguished Service Order and Bar and being awarded the American Silver Star which, owing to the pettiness of officialdom, he was not allowed to accept.

The original intention was that Blow and his party should parachute on to the peninsula behind Semporna on the east coast, but he decided that it would be more practical if the party went in by armed launch. This they did on 14 July and landed undetected at Semporna. Blow had with him Corporal Koram of the North Borneo Constabulary who had helped him to escape two years earlier from Berhala Island, a Sikh, Pretam Singh, and a Bajau, Abdul Karim. All of them were on the Japanese wanted list, having carried out a number of successful ambushes in which many Japanese had been killed.

The main tasks allotted to Agas IV were to find out how many Japanese there were in the area, what they were doing, the state of their armament and their health and anything else which would be of use to the Allied invading force. This meant moving all over the Semporna peninsula and up and down the coast from Tawau to Mostyn and across the bay to Lahad Datu where Major J. Maclaren, commanding Agas V, was operating.

The launch was heavily armed with a 20mm cannon in the bows, a .50 calibre machine-gun in the stern and Bren guns on either side. Using their boat, Major Blow and his party moved about the area trying, among other things, to incite the Japanese to action, but they seemed to prefer a quiet life even when Blow and his men flew over their posts at treetop height in Catalina flying boats hurling grenades from the open gun blisters. They did, however, manage to get some reaction on one occasion when reconnoitring a hemp plantation. Corporal Koram, Pretam Singh and Abdul Karim left the launch by canoe at the mouth of a river leading to the plantation and paddled upstream with instructions to find out how many Japanese were on the plantation. They were to rendezvous with the launch next evening at the river mouth. At the appointed hour the launch was in position when the three appeared, paddling frantically and close on their heels came several boatloads of infuriated Japanese. It transpired that they had been unable to resist throwing grenades into a group of Japanese officers playing cards in a house. The launch went into action and the Japanese were blasted so comprehensively that not a man escaped.

When news was received that the war was over, Corporal Koram was broken-hearted because he was not allowed to kill any more Japanese and took a very poor view of the several bargeloads of Japanese who arrived at Semporna to surrender.

Agas V, the final phase, commanded by Major J. Maclaren, was landed in the area of Lahad Datu on 27 July, 1945, and operated until 10 September, establishing a good and efficient network of agents which gave much valuable information.

Unlike Semut, Agas had the problem of operating in coastal areas under considerable pressure and their achievements were therefore all the more notable. If there had been a co-ordinated link-up with Semut the results from both their operations would have been considerably improved.

Both Agas and Semut were greatly helped by three officers at Services Reconnaissance Department's headquarters in Melbourne. Colonel J. Finlay, the Director of Plans, was a Camberley-trained Staff Officer, a most intelligent and consistently helpful man; Major Courtney, already an old hand at subversive operations in the European theatre, was an enthusiastic GSO 2; finally, as GSO 3, there was a Major Crowther, in peacetime an oilfield surveyor, whose attention to detail made both Agas and Semut really operable.

Semut

Harrisson's opposite number in Semut was Major G. C. Carter, a colleague of Crowther's in prewar oilfield surveying who knew the Baram-Tinjar River basin which the Oxford expedition had traversed in 1932 very well. A New Zealander, he had been through the New Guinea campaign with an army unit before being absorbed into Z Special. Both he and Crowther had already thought out a fairly detailed plan for entry into West Borneo.

This first plan was based on the insertion of the Semut group by submarine. This particularly appealed to Carter as he did not much like the idea of a drop in by parachute, but on examination many snags appeared. In the first place it was known that the Japanese were concentrated along the coast; then there was the need for the submarine to stay well out from the shore to avoid coral reefs and submerged rocks, which meant landing by boat, with subsequent difficulties of loading and unloading in fluctuating tides and winds, to say nothing of being sitting targets while crossing mud flats; the third point was that, even if a submarine landing was achieved it would be very difficult for the party to move from the coast to a location of reasonable security and then set up a long-term operation suitable for passing back information and later helping the landing of regular troops in Borneo.

The coastal people were, in the main, Chinese or Mohammedan Malays and were very much under Japanese eyes; but the inland people, the Kenyahs, Kayans and others, were devoted to white men, a result of the goodwill built up during a century of Rajah Brooke's rule. Further inland there were a people called by the overall name of the Kelabits. All this led Harrisson to carry out some research in the Melbourne Library and he found his reward in a 1911 issue of the *Sarawak Museum Journal*. There, in a report by R. O. Douglas entitled 'An Expedition into the Bah Country', he found, inter alia, this description:

In front and below us there was stretched out a great plain. This great plain . . . must be about 2-3 thousand feet above sea level . . . It had been thoroughly irrigated and was covered with crops . . . All the tribes beyond the Tamabo range are entirely self-supporting.

In 1937, while curator of the Sarawak Museum, Mr E. Banks had written a report which supported this information:

Lam Bah is a small village of not more than fifty people immensely rich in this world's goods thanks to their situation. The plain itself is as flat as a board covered with long grass or scrub where it is not cultivated and I can scarcely imagine a more ideal spot for European occupation if only more accessible.

The name Kelabit was due to a misunderstanding. In the early 1900s a District Officer named Hose, on tour in the Baram area, asked his so-called interpreter at the government station near the mouth of the Baram River to find out from a man from the uplands to what race he belonged. The interpreter said that he was from the 'Pa Labid' people (i.e. the Labid river people: Pa means a river). Hose misheard and said,

'Ah, the Kalabit.'

Ever since, the name has been used to cover the host of different people inhabiting the interior of Borneo and Sarawak, despite the fact that there are the Kenyahs, the Kayans, the Bisaya (noted for their skill in sorcery and magic), the Bawang, the Tagals, the Punans and the Ibans and others. However, the word is now spelt Kelabit.

While Harrisson was gathering this information, the

Right A hut being built for the Australians on Timor –
Pte J Williams, Sgt AE Smith, Pte A Elder, Pte C Chopping.
Photograph: Australian War Memorial

Below left On Patrol: Cpl Sargent, Pte J Williams, Pte C Chopping, Pte WA Crossing, Sgt AE Smith.
Photograph: Australian War Memorial

Below right Lt-Col AL Spence, Lt E Smyth, Major BJ Callinan.
Photograph: Australian War Memorial

Right Colonel BJ Callinan.
Photograph: Australian War Memorial

Below Operation Jaywick team.
Back row: Berryman, Marsh, Jones, Huston. *Centre:* Crilley, Cain, McDowell, Young, Falls, Morris. *Front:* Carse, Davidson, Lyon, Major Campbell (not a member of the team), Page.
Photograph: Australian War Memorial

Above 'Winnie the War Winner.'
Photograph: Australian War Memorial

Right A member of the Jaywick team beside a two-man Folboat hidden in the thick jungle.
Photograph: Australian War Memorial

MV *Krait*. Length 70ft, speed 6½ knots, range in normal circumstances 8000 miles. Photograph taken in Hawkesbury River, New South Wales, during training. *Photograph: Australian War Memorial*

Major Lyon at the forward observation post on the north side of Dongas Island from which the Singapore Roads and Keppel Harbour were clearly visible. *Photograph: Australian War Memorial*

Men of the Jaywick team 'blacking up' before the raid on Singapore.
Photograph: Australian War Memorial

Men of the 2/2 Company Headquarters at Ailalec, Timor. *Photograph: Australian War Memorial*

Nomadic Punans who served as erratic blowpipe units in 1945. *Photograph: Tom Harrisson*

HMAS *Tigersnake*. Lt WK Witt, RANVR, and crew *en route* to Long Akah, Borneo. *Photograph: WK Witt*

HMS *Porpoise* prior to use in Operation Rimau. *Photograph: Imperial War Museum*

HMAS *Tigersnake* of Services Reconnaissance Department's special craft. Taken at Darwin 1944. *Photograph: RAAF*

Careening Bay, West Australia. The training headquarters for Services Reconnaissance Department's amphibious operations. *Photograph: West Australian Newspapers*

Wreck of HMAS *Voyager,* AD Stevenson in centre.

third member of Semut arrived in Melbourne. Major W. Sochon had been recruited by Egerton Mott because he had served in the police force under the third Rajah Brooke of Sarawak. The Brooke family had always been apt to employ and discharge staff in an arbitrary manner and one day, some years before the war, for no apparent reason Sochon was politely but firmly transferred out of the Sarawak service. An ex-Commissioner of Prisons, he was a large, cheerful man, had been through the SOE schools in England and always felt that he had been treated very meanly. This was an opportunity to justify himself. In fact, both he and Tom Harrisson had scores to settle.

Despite Harrisson's researches it was difficult to come by information about the interior of what was then Dutch Borneo (now Kalimantan) but here again the Gods looked favourably on the venture and, through the help of Brigadier-General Knox, a previous director of Military Intelligence in the Australian Army, and a feat of organization by Z Special and the Shell company, Dr W. F. Schneeberger, a high-ranking geologist who had explored the north-west interior of Dutch Borneo for Shell just before the war and had spent nearly a year in the area, was contacted and confirmed Harrisson's library researches that there were:

1. Plenty of pagan people.
2. Plenty of food on the grassland, especially rice.
3. Jungle tracks from the interior to the coast which were practicable but difficult.
4. Virtually no direct contact between the coast and the plains.

Apart from providing much information, Dr Schneeberger confirmed that there was no way of distinguishing between Sarawak and the territories of North and South Borneo on the ground in the interior because surveys had either not been completed or were non-existent. He also suggested that needles and fish hooks would make better currency than notes. As a result Z, with its usual profusion, provided, for the first landing at Bario, fifty thousand fish hooks and a quarter of a million needles. In due course the demand was satisfied and the needles were incorporated in jungle palisades set to guard camps at night and proved to be very effective.

The accumulation of all this information and its inferences finally won over the planners, Carter and Sochon, to the insertion of Semut by parachute. It was necessary to recruit Australians to make up each section of Semut and the obvious place to find them was among the Australian army paratroops. The wide area for selection gave Harrisson the opportunity to select men who fitted in best with what Z required – a capability to cope with the unorthodox when the situation required and to be able to lead men and to control them.

The problem then was to fly over the interior of Borneo to choose an area into which to drop. This proved to be very difficult since the Americans had overall superiority in all things military and MacArthur's strategy did not include any 'sideshows' during his island-hopping advance towards Japan. However, Z training was geared to getting what it wanted and, after many exhausting and frustrating weeks, Harrisson and Squadron-Leader Cook, RAAF, by a judicious distribution of six-chambered Smith and Wesson revolvers, which all right-thinking Americans treasured far above their large Browning automatics, managed to get permission to use some of a USN Search Liberator's time to examine the interior of Borneo in the vicinity of the area in which they hoped to drop later.

The Liberator was being sent to look for a US Navy Bomber which had failed to return from an attack on Japanese shipping off Labuan Island and its flight was scheduled to cross the middle of Borneo on its way back to base. The crew of the Liberator were due to fly back to the United States the next day and, although very careful to make sure that they came back in one piece, they gave Harrisson and Cook a generous amount of time.

There was no sign of the crashed bomber, so, under Harrisson's direction, the Liberator turned behind Brunei Bay and headed in the general direction of a beautiful, white, twin-pinnacled mountain with a saddle joining its peaks. This was identified as Batu Lawi, its pinnacles the male and female symbols of all upland people, whose existence was saved, so tradition has it, by the couple defeating the mountain of fire, Batu Apoi, which was intent on consuming them in its inferno. At first there was no sign of a suitable dropping ground as the Liberator cruised along on a course a little south of east, but suddenly, after crossing an impressive double range, a deep valley opened up showing in its centre several miles of grassland. The pilot was getting worried about his fuel reserve, but as they turned for base Cook managed to get a photograph which later showed several square miles of ground without a single tree.

Their enterprise was rewarded, for the project at once gained credibility and prestige, and a second flight, during which the cloud was thinner, enabled Harrisson to see several large, clear, flat places under extensive cultivation and in due course their first drop was on one of these places near Batu Lawi which, they were to discover, was called the Plain of Bah.

The machinations of Z Special had now become sufficiently acknowledged for the Semut parties to be able to use Liberators allocated to Z. They had been adapted for dropping agents and stores by inserting a large tube inclined at an angle and fitted forward of the camera hatch near the tail. Unlike drops from a Whitley (mind your

head against the other side of the hole) or from the door
of a Douglas (step well out and mind the tail plane) the
chute on the Liberator involved the parachutist in nothing
worse than a slide down a smooth tube – and then the
sensation of floating in the 200 mph slipstream until the
static line ran out and the parachute opened. After that
there were a few tense moments concentrating on man-
oeuvring the parachute, remembering the landing drill
and actually landing without, if possible, breaking or
straining anything. It was through the inclined tube that
Semut made its debut in 1945 on to the Plain of Bah.

Harrisson had selected two groups for the initial drop:
in his own group he had Staff-Sergeant Sanderson, AIF,
Staff-Sergeant Bower, AIF, and Sergeant Barry, AIF.
Sanderson was chosen for a previous knowledge of the
east, though not of Borneo, a facility for language,
courage, quick intelligence and a disregard for personal
comfort. His special responsibility was to make the earliest possible contact with the locals and to try to arrange
help to gather up the several tons of stores to be dropped
after insertion.

Bower was the radio operator and mechanic; a man of
even temperament and willing to tackle anything, his
immediate concern was to recover the radio, reassemble it
and contact Darwin as soon as possible.

Barry, in civilian life a surveyor, was an experienced
soldier and a good organizer. Small and very strong, his
first job was to organize the collection of the stores
dropped.

Harrisson, in keeping with Z Special style, had been
allowed to select whoever he liked as his second-in-
command and had chosen Captain E. Edmeades, NZF,
who was the senior instructor in the Australian Parachute
School and had carried out more jumps than anyone on
the continent. He was also quite unlike Harrisson in that

he believed in toughness for its own sake and took risks for fun. He never accepted that anything was impossible and everything he did was done at least twice as fast and as well as could be expected. Harrisson had also chosen him for another reason: he considered, and rightly, that there would be personal problems with the Australian subordinates in the party and that Edmeades would be a better man, both as a New Zealander and on account of his considerable prestige in the Australian Army, to sort them out. This later proved correct.

With Edmeades there was Sergeant Hallam, AIF, as the second wireless operator, Staff-Sergeant Tredea, AIF, a medical orderly whose sympathetic outlook and clear desire to help people suffering from lack of medical attention was to do much to establish Semut, and Warrant Officer Cusack, AIF, a tall, cool, quiet Queenslander, who was the quartermaster.

Flight 200 was commanded by Squadron Leader Graham Pockley DSO DFC, RAAF, who was already renowned for his anti-submarine work off south-west England, and it was from his Liberator that Harrisson and his group slid out into the low cloud of a Borneo morning over the Bario area and landed ·in a swamp which they later learned was inhabited by a very large King Cobra responsible for killing six buffaloes. It was also full of ticks carrying scrub typhus.

Inevitably the disciplined landing and immediate action so frequently and carefully rehearsed on the Queensland Downs went completely awry and the party floundered about trying to locate each other and the 'Storpedoes' (cylinders as long as a man, made from hard cardboard reinforced with metal strips, with a conical head and at the rear end a strong coarse cloth parachute. The nose struck the ground first and took up the shock and in this way it was possible to drop large quantities of all kinds of stores with safety).

No one in the party had been hurt in the drop and Sanderson set off immediately to try to contact the local people. Soon there appeared out of the morning mist what seemed to be a small white flag. It turned out to be a small piece of white linen tied to the end of a long, polished blow pipe and was held by an olive-skinned man with long, black hair reaching below his waist. The party made encouraging noises and squelched over to make contact. The man was shivering as much from the morning cold as from fear, and first attempts with bastard Malay were not promising, but the production of cigarettes and matches had a magical effect. Later on Harrisson learnt that he was Amat, the son of Chief Lawai Bisarai, and thought that they were reproving him for not bringing them any borak (the local fermented drink) and was terribly ashamed.

Bower was left to search for the radio and other stores and the man, soon joined by two others, led Harrisson and Barry out of the swamp and on to a plain whose clean, dry grassland was alive with the song of sedge and reed warblers. As the sun came up over the eastern ranges they could see that they were in a beautiful valley and they soon reached a long house set on a knoll at the edge of the plain at the foot of steep mountain slopes covered with thick jungle.

The entrance to the long house was at the top of a long notched pole, slippery and difficult to climb. Waiting at the top of it was the Chief Penghulu Lawai Bisarai. He was magnificent in a leopardskin hat, hornbill feathers, beads, brass earrings, a sword in an embroidered sheath, leg bangles and – relic of the Rajah Brooke era – a tattered khaki coat. Their welcome had already been prepared by the skill with which Sanderson, using sign language, had explained that they had come to fight the Japanese and that there were many stores out on the plain waiting to be gathered up.

There followed a period of some confusion while the initial shyness melted and the borak flowed. It appeared that for some months past the occasional aircraft had caused increasing alarm. It seemed as though the spirits which they worshipped might be contemplating a return to the plain and it was likely that they would need propitiating with supplies of borak, rice, pork and women. Now the people wanted to know whether the group were humans, and how did they get out of the aeroplane? Harrisson was anxious to know whether there were any Japanese in the area and would Penghulu Lawai's people help the party?

Sanderson soon made them understand that the first essential was to find the storpedoes and, under Barry and Bower, parties set out to search the plain, while Harrisson and Sanderson sat drinking with Penghulu Lawai. Within an hour – and it was a very brave thing to do – the Penghulu had pledged himself and his people to help, but, he asked, would the party back him up against the Japanese? They could and they would, replied Harrisson, and soon, he said, there would be further drops of supplies. By now the borak was having an effect and Harrisson was beginning to worry about the second party, under Edmeades.

Meanwhile the storpedoes were being collected. It took eight or nine strong Kelabits to carry each one, but when they discovered that there were panels of khaki cloth attached to them, the rate of search redoubled, for since the Japanese invasion the supply of cloth from the coast had stopped and the Kelabits had had to revert to bark cloth which was not to their liking.

Towards dusk the uneasy feelings about the safety of the other four were relieved by loud shouts across the plain as the second party was guided towards Bario. Edmeades had seen the first four jump, so he and his stick had jumped at the same time, crashing down on the jungle canopy three miles from the dropping zone. Two had crashed straight through the trees; the other two had used their ropes and harness to get down from the canopy. Once they reached the ground it had taken them two hours to find each other and they had then navigated by compass on the basis of a rough sketch made by Harrisson before the flight. Their storpedoes, funnily enough, landed in the right place.

As soon as Edmeades's group was in the long house the real party began and it became clear that, even if there were any Japanese in the area, no one was in a mood to care. The borak flowed fast and songs and dances, including a rendering of 'Three Blind Mice' by the Semut parties, went on through the night until at last the whole long house fell asleep, undisturbed by the packs of dogs prowling about inside the house and eating whatever they could find, including Sergeant Cusack's much-prized self-winding watch.

Next morning the borak haze had lifted sufficiently to allow the wireless operators to get their aerial erected on the knoll overlooking the long house and to begin pumping out the call sign on the reserved frequency on which Darwin was keeping a twenty-four-hour watch. Next came the implementation of the five basic tasks.

a. To reconnoitre a way west for the second party led by Carter and Sochon to follow, and to ensure their good reception by the Kenyahs and Kayans.

b. To find out more about the area to the east, vital if operations were to extend rapidly.

c. To reconnoitre northwards into Brunei Bay to get intelligence about the Japanese forces there.

d. If the probe to the east proved practicable, to find out as much as possible about Japanese positions on the mainland opposite Tarakan Island which was to be the first Allied objective on the east coast.

e. There had been reports in Australia of large numbers of Australian, Dutch and other prisoners-of-war who had escaped into the interior; a special effort was to be made to locate and, if possible, rescue them. They were thought to be somewhere in the hills near Tarakan.

Harrisson decided to send Tredea and Cusack into that area, Sanderson towards Brunei Bay and Edmeades and Barry westwards to reconnoitre the Baram area. Within forty-eight hours Edmeades and Barry had left to climb the Tamabo mountains and make the long journey down the outer side of the mountain bowl to Kubaan, then through the forests to try and contact the river people on the Akah tributary of the main Baram.

The other parties had to wait since there was too much to do locally and one of the first bits of information that they got came from Penghulu Miri who appeared on the second day. He had taken his name from the first great oil centre in British Borneo, when, under the Brooke régime, he had been made Penghulu of the southern Kelabits. He spoke fluent Malay and was emphatic that there were no large groups of Europeans anywhere in the interior but there were some individual whites scattered about – men who had crashed their aircraft in or behind Brunei Bay and escaped inland. Some had been caught and beheaded, some were ill and were being looked after by the local people.

The morning of the second day also saw the arrival of numerous deputations from the surrounding long houses. They had put on their best clothes and were greeted formally by Chief Lawai. Penghulu Miri, whose real name was Rajah Omong ('Above all rajahs'), urged Harrisson to go south and see his territory at Pa Dali before deciding on a permanent headquarters, or at least to make an alternative headquarters there in case the Japanese got on his track, and this was arranged as soon as Cusack had

sorted out his stores in Bario. Penghulu Miri also exhorted
them not to make their base in the east but to stay in
Sarawak, because its loyalty to the Brookes would make it
100% loyal to Semut. And, of course, though he did not
say so, it would enhance his own prestige *vis-à-vis* the
other chiefs.

By the second evening Bower got through to Darwin
(the wireless transmitter and receiver had been moved to
the crest of the bowl to avoid the blanketing effects of the
bowl) and the feeling of isolation vanished. One factor
which had increased the prestige of the men who had
'dropped from the sky' was the unpacking of the rifles,
carbines, Sten guns, hand grenades etc. from the storpedoes. The male population went wild. Were they really
going to be allowed to use these lethal weapons? The
Japanese had taken all their shotguns and the enthusiasm
for reprisals, while very gratifying, made Harrisson rather
uneasy at the prospect of controlling hordes of basically
savage warriors. But he put the thought aside for the time
being; nowhere near enough supplies had yet been dropped in and the people could see this.

Nevertheless the result was that Edmeades and his
party had immediate and very willing volunteers to go
over the mountains with them to act as runners (and
gunners if possible).

In the Bario long house that second evening the five
great chiefs of the uplands assembled – Aran Tuan of
Pa Trap, Tama Bulan of P'Umur, Ngomong Sakai of Pa
Main, Penghulu Miri and Penghulu Lawai of Bisarai.
They talked among themselves far into the night, planning
the maximum assistance to Semut. Harrisson, on the edge
of the group, found himself in the morning much borak-
anointed and, because of the gold major's crown in his
cap, regarded as a Rajah. This was very gratifying but led
to trouble later.

Edmeades and Barry had five main jobs to do, mostly concerning the assessment of support Semut would receive from the Kenyahs and Kayans. In due course Edmeades would return to report, leaving Barry to maintain a presence. In the meantime the other six members of Semut I were given tasks which filled their days to the full. Bower and Hallam were to establish regular contact with Darwin; Cusack was to distribute stores and deal with the general administration, then to set up an alternative emergency camp at Pa Dali, Penghulu Miri's headquarters; Tredea was to tour all adjoining long houses and give medical treatment, spreading the maximum goodwill; Sanderson was to concentrate on obtaining and recording all possible information about adjacent people and affairs. Everyone was to become proficient in the local languages, practise movement in difficult country, and learn to live off it independent of stores.

The main camp had to be moved. The long house at Bario was quite unsuitable as a headquarters, owing to the lack of privacy and the danger of losing valuable equipment through the ravages of dogs. Harrisson also wanted to be able to receive and talk to people in privacy, especially since news of their arrival had spread rapidly to surrounding areas and groups either hostile to or unfamiliar with the Kelabits were coming in with offers of help. Such were the Bawang people who had been wrongly and rather fiercely treated by a Brooke punitive expedition some years before.

The best track down to Brunei Bay led through their territory but it had been closed to Kelabits for many years and that meant a ten-day diversion by way of Kubaan into the headwaters of the Limbang. Two things contributed to easing this problem: a special supply drop of arms was arranged and carried out with such precision that the Kelabits and others were convinced that the 'Rajah' and his myrmidons were indeed supported from on high; also the arrival of two outstanding leaders. The first, Penghulu Badak (Great Rhinoceros) was the chief of the Kelabits, Muruts, Tabuns and related peoples living in the upper stretches of the Limbang to the north-west and within comparatively easy reach of Brunei Town by river. The other, Lasong Piri, was chief of the Bawang and all related peoples to the east and one of the most influential men inside Borneo.

There was some initial difficulty in persuading these two powerful figures to lay aside their traditional animosity for the time being but Harrisson accomplished it and so cleared the way for the use of the tracks down to Brunei through the Bawang territory by non-Bawang people. The two men were somewhat similar physically but their outlooks reflected the different attitudes of the Brooke and the Dutch administrations to the areas under their control.

The Brookes had made a point of leaving the people under their control alone as much as possible and, although they demanded a reasonable respect for law and order, they kept outside influences from harming the people. Their rule was based on affection, not on discipline, and as a result Badak never raised one problem, one difficulty or one hesitation from the moment he pledged himself. He was a short, tough, smiling man with the heart of a lion. Though he was within Japanese contact he declared himself openly for Semut and the Allies and though his people suffered as a result, he remained unflinching throughout the difficult times that were to follow.

The Dutch, on the other hand, had their part of Borneo better organized, but for their own profit; it was a colonial system which ignored the pride and dignity of people who were not Dutch by birth or who did not have a Dutch father. Lasong Piri had been brought up under this régime and as a consequence was a much more difficult person to deal with than Badak. Badak treated Harrisson as a respected equal provided that he lived up to his 'Rajah' expectations, but Lasong Piri started by treating him as a distant superior and only later, with great difficulty, came to like him.

The loyalties of Badak and Lasong Piri provided an opportunity for the projected reconnaissances to get off the mark more quickly than had at first seemed possible, so Harrisson, taking Cusack with him, set off to cover the area of the southern Kelabits. Heavy rain did not dampen the enthusiasm of the 100,000 or so people who, voluntarily, wished to join Semut. Harrisson was in a quandary. Could their presence be kept secret from the Japanese at least until Semut II was in position? As it happened, he need not have worried for three things tipped the scales strongly in their favour.

Firstly, the Japanese, as usual, had behaved with incredible stupidity in showing even more contempt for the inland people than they had for the Malays on the coast or latterly for the Dutch. Secondly, they had brought much of the commerce of the island to a standstill. Thirdly, the people of the interior were fighting men. They admired boldness and physical bravery in combat and this had been denied them for many years, albeit with their own reluctant consent, and now they had an opportunity to establish themselves once more in their own eyes and in the eyes of outsiders as warriors. What better target than the loathed Japanese?

Harrisson's unease was mitigated by the return of Edmeades, who had already been nicknamed 'Lightning' by the local people. He came back from his visit to the territory of the Kenyahs and Kayans to report that he had contacted Weng Ajang, the great chief of the lowlands, who had shown a readiness to help as great as that of

Penghulu Lawai of Bisarai and he felt sure that the
Kenyahs would give Semut II their full support.

All was now arranged for the arrival of Semut II and
Harrisson sat on the knoll beside the long house at Bario
and watched the drops. The two Liberators came over and
dropped four men in the first run and twelve storpedoes in
the second. The second plane then came in and did
likewise.

Carter, who disliked parachuting, made a perfect landing, as did all the others except Sochon. He weighed
something over 14 stone and the parachutes allocated to Z
Special had already been used over 100 times. As they
would not be recoverable it was reckoned that anything
else would be a waste. There was probably also an
element of jealousy from the regular Australian Army
parachutists who had never become operational.

As Sochon dropped, Harrisson watched the panels
leave his parachute with a high-pitched ping. What
Sochon thought is best expressed in his own words:

I looked up to see that my 'chute was properly opened and that I
had not developed twists or that my rigging lines were not caught
up, when, to my horror, I discovered that seven of my parachute
panels were ripped from top to bottom and as I fell through the
sky fourteen panels in all ripped from top to bottom.

However, fortune was with him and he landed in the
swamp. Otherwise he would have been smashed to pieces.
This resulted in a vituperative signal to base and thereafter all bodies dropped in had new, cream-coloured silk
parachutes. When the men and stores had been gathered
in, Harrisson, Carter and Sochon went into conference
and there followed a difficult three days sorting out
seniorities and communications. The country was extremely tough from the point of view of communications
and it could delay and endanger a project if everything

had to be referred to Darwin through one channel. Finally a sensible solution was agreed upon and blessed by Darwin. Harrisson was given control of the uplands and all the country north of Brunei Bay; Carter was to take over all the country west of the Tamabo in the Sarawak lowlands as Semut II, and Sochon took over the area beyond the Baram watershed into the great Rajang River system further south as Semut III. Harrisson now began to move his main camp and wireless station across the plain to Pa Mein, staying there long enough to consolidate his arrangements and organize a system of contacts, before moving on, and avoiding numerous and kindly attempts, mostly borak-inspired at 'iraus' (death feasts), to provide him with 'wives'. He finally came by fortunate accident to settle down in the best place of all.

He had reached Lembudut, accompanied by an ever-increasing retinue, to find Tredea in occupation and there they awaited a drop of men and arms. The fires were lit, the smoke signals started and two Liberators came over. Then, to everyone's astonishment, they headed north. There was nothing to do but wait and see what happened, a wait enlivened by another brew offered by the chief of the Lembudut people. In the middle of a pleasant time being had by all, there arrived a panting runner from a very aggrieved Lieutenant Westley saying that he and his men and stores were down and awaiting collection. But where were they? Harrisson and his entourage set out in the hot sun to cross the low divide north of Lembudut. They marched for hours, gradually frying out and larding the earth with their borak. At long last they came out on a glorious, open rice plain, the finest of them all, running from the head of the Bawang under Mount Murud eastwards to Belawit and on past the rich mineral springs of Pa Potok.

Westley and his seven men were surrounded by several

thousand wellwishers and they and their stores were comfortably ensconced in a long house. It appeared that there had been a pilot error but it was clear that this was the ideal place for a headquarters – a plain arranged by nature for a dropping zone and one on which an airstrip could be built. It was, in fact, the plain Harrisson had seen in Dr Schneeberger's photographs in Melbourne – and the reality was even better. From then on the Bawang valley and Balawit in particular became the centre of all Semut I operations.

However, the Gods had directed Harrisson and his party to drop at Bario in the first place, for they knew that the Japanese sent frequent patrols into the Bawang area and the large population, which was in constant communication with the east coast, had not *initially* been very sympathetic to the white man. Now they were completely won over and became very Semut-minded, so much so that the Japanese began to find that their supplies of rice, buffaloes, salt and conscripted labour, which had come down the river valleys, no longer did so. But from the beginning to the end of the campaign, when the guerrillas struck at the Japanese in support of the Allied landings, not one of all the thousands of Borneo people involved with Semut betrayed them and the Japanese never had any proof of their existence.

The next task was to build an airstrip, since Harrisson now felt that he had sufficient support to risk the Japanese finding it. He had also, through Sanderson, Tredea and others, managed to collect thirteen shot-down American airmen who he wanted to return to their bases as soon as possible. They had been found in all stages of sickness and disrepair and some had to be carried by stretcher over the mountains to the Bawang valley where they could be properly nursed. They were all very young and blissfully unaware of any other country than their own, so much so that they wondered why they could not be provided with Chesterfield cigarettes and American newspapers immediately.

Harrisson asked for equipment to perfect his airfield and forty-eight hours later the plain was bombarded with an agricultural rain of picks, hoes, shovels, rakes, graders, etc., dropped by the American Airforce. However, the conservative locals preferred their ancient method of breaking ground with sticks and trampling it into shape, and in ten days an excellent strip had been constructed on the sandy side of the plain. Alongside it Sergeant Long and Private Griffiths set up their radio and radar station, while Harrisson made his headquarters some 600 yards away on the edge of the plain near some long houses, keeping contact with Sergeant Long by first attracting his attention with shots from a carbine and then coming up on the air on a walkie-talkie.

The departure of the airmen came when Lieutenant Cheyney, RAAF, flew in in an Australian Auster from Tarakan, a Brigade of the Australian task force having landed there on 1 May, 1945. Tarakan was just about due east of Balawit across very unpleasant and stormy country but, if fuel was dropped in to Balawit, an Auster could manage the distance. The landing was perfect but Cheyncy was dubious about the length of the strip for take off. Harrisson, filled with bravado and to show the Americans that all was well, took off with him on the first flight. The Auster ended nose up in the mud. Within three days Penghulu Lasong Piri and his men had lengthened the strip by another 100 yards and surfaced it with bamboo. The second Auster flew in; repairs were made to the first one and the strip thereafter was regarded as superior to that at Tarakan, which was subject to flood. It was probably the only bamboo strip ever built.

The presence of Australian troops on the coast opened

new contacts and responsibilities and Harrisson flew down to be received by Brigadier D. Whitehead of Desert Rat fame. The information Semut had sent out had been most helpful, especially a reconnaissance of Tarakan Island itself, carried out by Captain Prentice, AIF, an Australian captain in Z Special. Harrisson's sudden emergence on the coast stirred the Z Special staff on Morotai to unusual activity and he flew there for a discussion with Major Campbell, now in charge and well supported by Courtney, Finlay and Crowther. The visit enabled much to be done which would otherwise have taken weeks to arrange over the wireless and Harrisson was able to take back with him a number of picked men who had been brought forward to Morotai ready to be dropped anywhere at short notice. One in particular was to be of great help to him. Captain J.Blondeel was Flemish and already greatly experienced with SOE in Europe. Unlike other European officers in service with SOE and sent on to Force 136, he had the ability to see the point of view of the local people and was able to modify the sometimes harsh outlook of those who had been used to cloak-and-dagger activities in Europe.

Australian large-scale landings were to be made on 10 June at Labuan and Semut I, II and III were all now supplying intelligence of Japanese positions and activities on the mainland and in the coastal areas. In general Semut had to prepare positions behind Brunei Bay and, more widely, to enable them to synchronize positive attacks from behind the Japanese lines with the seaborne landings. They would also disrupt Japanese communications and in general do what they could to hamper the enemy.

The Semut strategy was to get at the Japanese before they stumbled across Semut; this was done by air strikes on groups of Japanese in the jungle and particularly those using the navigable rivers such as the Sembakong. It soon became clear that the Japanese were moving towards a major defensive position – north-east from the west coast and north and north-north-east from the east coast. Semut was under strict orders not to attack nor to carry out any dislocation until D-day, 10 June, but already there were signs that the Japanese were getting restless and angry. This was in considerable measure due to the drying-up of their supplies of rice, cattle, salt and labour from the interior, but the full effect was delayed for some weeks because of the tactics of Bigar Anak Debois, their Native Officer in Administration.

He was a land Dayak from Kuching far away in the south-west corner of Sarawak and had been an experienced junior administrative officer under the Brookes. The Japanese had posted him to Lawas on the edge of Brunei Bay and, because he spoke several dialects fluently, had come to rely on him to a large extent. Semut had had good accounts of him soon after they dropped in; he had protected and helped the Christian missionaries heading up the Trusan River soon after the Japanese arrived; he had also acted as an effective go-between in many cases of hardship and possible torture and murder, and had succeeded in alleviating and sometimes cancelling punishments.

Early on Harrisson had selected a special agent from Bario to contact Bigar and inform him of the existence of Semut. This contact was successful and led to Edmeades moving down the Trusan towards Lawas and Brunei Bay. The excellent Murut headman, Kerus, unhesitatingly looked after him and, using Lieutenant Pinkerton, AIF, and Sergeant W. Nibbs, AIF, a small base was built up. Edmeades contacted Bigar first via an intermediary and then by direct meeting in the jungle. The result of this liaison was outstanding. Bigar could pass on information fed to him and provide Harrisson with secret Japanese messages sent over the radio. He was also able to provide the Japanese with individuals from the uplands who had been carefully rehearsed in stories explaining why their supplies were drying up.

By the time excuses such as floods, droughts, disease, deaths of great chiefs and plagues of birds and rats had all been used the suspicions of the Japanese were thoroughly roused and they could not be prevented from sending a punitive force into the uplands to deal with the 'dirty savages' and make sure they toed the line without further delay. Bigar provided precise information of the plan, including numbers, equipment and routes, and, as Harrisson said, it was really unfair, almost unsporting. The Japanese must not be annihilated too near the coast nor must they be allowed to travel too far inland, in case they learnt secrets. So the ambush must be set at exactly the right place, and the Muruts and Kelabits, who were itching to use their newly acquired weapons, must be restrained – one shot could spoil the whole ambush.

The patrol was allowed to get seven days up the Trusan River and the ambush was set where the path climbs steeply out of the creek above Long Semadoh. The signal was a shout and a large, concentrated and lethal blast of fire was then unleashed at the Japanese at the rear of the patrol, since, following their custom, they had put their Javanese carriers at the front carrying wooden firearms. The Japanese were wiped out and the terrified Javanese, after being kindly treated and given proper food, later settled down to make tracks and bridges and to cultivate excellent gardens. One thing made them less than perfect – they appeared to be 90% kleptomaniacs and could not be trusted with any stores, perhaps because of their suffering under the Japanese.

The 100% success of this ambush greatly increased the already high morale of the guerrillas and the other ambushes that followed showed that they could be controlled and could, on most occasions, control themselves. Of all the Borneo people the Kelabits made the best soldiers, followed by the Muruts and the interrelated Potoks and Milaus; then the Kenyahs who came late to the fair but proved their worth under their leaders, Tama Weng Ajang and Tama Weng Tingang. Among the best fighters, but very hard to control because they were individualist and not used to tribal discipline, were the Ibans, who tended to take heads whenever they could and ask questions afterwards. They were perhaps the only Borneo people who preferred frontal attacks and later their bravery earned them a deservedly high reputation with British troops in Malaya.

By this time Harrisson had over 1,000 armed men in simple uniform under his control with another thousand even more irregular troops armed with shotguns and other ancient weapons. There was, however, one problem and that was what to do with the Punans. They lived beyond the Kerayan River in the Toeboe and related river areas and were most anxious to help, but they were very wild nomadic people, inexperienced in even the simplest things and Harrisson thought it best not to arm them. They lived off wild vegetables and game and roamed in small groups over wide areas and did not, normally, have anything to do with the world outside their own fastnesses; but they did need two things – tobacco and iron – and for these they traded their own beautiful black and white mats and baskets. The advent of the Japanese dried up their sources of supply and they felt strongly the necessity to kill any Japanese they could.

They used blow pipes and poisoned darts in their hunting and were masters of silent movement and tracking. When they offered their services, they were put loosely under the command of the local Semut officer. The operations they carried out were all completely succesful. There was, for instance, the ambush of a Japanese group near Malinau behind Tarakan, while they were wading a river. The Japanese were picked off by poisoned darts and died in great agony, not knowing what had hit them. Blow pipes are virtually silent – just a slight sibilant puff – and if the first dart misses it is easy to pump in several more in rapid succession.

Now, as the tide began to turn against the Japanese, they began to suffer desertions from local conscripts. One of the first of these was Chong Ah Onn, previously a medical dresser in the Sarawak government. He had long chafed under the Japanese dictates and, when he heard that there were guerrillas at Lawas, he slipped away from his post and appeared at Lawas asking to join Semut. He was welcomed and sent to Harrisson who put him in charge of the newly erected hospital at Bawang, provided him with ample supplies and left him to carry on medical treatment on a scale of which he had dreamt for years.

Other recruits deserting from the Japanese were twenty Chinese who were formed into a group at Bawang and served with distinction all over the Semut area. Then Bigar, having been forewarned, left his job just before D-day and joined Harrisson in mid-June. He proved to be a Godsend, for neither Harrisson nor any of his staff had any administrative training and it was urgently necessary to control and record the outflow of material things, particularly arms; for when the fighting ended it would be necessary to restore law and order among a warrior people who had been allowed to revert to their earlier killing habits.

The 10th of June, 1945, was the day when the guerrillas were no longer alone. 23,553 men of the Australian 9th Division, 6,525 men of the Royal Australian Air Force and 1,254 US personnel landed in Brunei Bay, mainly on Labuan Island. During the fighting which followed Semut did their best to disrupt the Japanese from the rear. Their efforts were not of a world-shaking nature in strictly military terms, but in all three of their areas they caused massive disruption of communications and put the fear of God into the Japanese, who did not know from which direction they might be attacked, particularly at night.

There was nothing of the set piece about the attacks. At Lawas, for example, the Japanese officer in charge was shot and then finished off with a spear as he walked to the garden lavatory early in the morning.

By midday Lieutenant Pinkerton had taken over Lawas and raised the Union Jack; he was ably abetted further along the coast by Sergeant Sanderson and his 'private' army, while the efforts of Semut were forcefully carried on further to the north-east inside the territory of North Borneo by Warrant Officer MacPherson and Corporal Griffiths. That was really the territory of Agas under Major Combe but, as there had been more difficulty in raising guerrilla forces in that area than in the rest of Borneo, Semut had been given permission to move into the Agas area. Semut II and III were fortunate in that they were further away from orthodox militarism and could get on with the destruction of the enemy without legal interference – a factor which badly hampered Semut I until Colonel Leach, a New Zealander, appeared in the Z Camp, which, characteristically, had been sited on the best clifftop position with access to the best bathing beach at Labuan. Leach was the liaison officer between Z Special and the 9th Division and was instrumental in ironing out many awkward problems which arose when the regular Australian Army, advancing to liberate Borneo, found that there were already Australian warrant officers, sergeants and even privates competently running their own private wars. Such had been Z Special security that no one in the regular Army knew of their existence and naturally there were some unpleasant scenes when the Z Special operatives had to return, very unwillingly, to their original ranks in the Army. When such situations became really difficult Harrisson severed nearly all his contacts with the regular forces and retired into the interior where the Australian Army had decided not to go.

Semut III under Sochon was fortunate in having large navigable rivers in the Rajang area on which seaplanes could land. This enabled Harrisson and Courtney to fly down to his headquarters in an Iban long house on the Rajang River. Sochon's forces were largely Iban Sea Dayaks and his main difficulty was keeping them under control, but in this he was given aid by the insertion of Major Fisher, a tall, amiable and effective administrative officer of the Brooke era, who was able to sort out the problems left behind as Sochon and his warriors, pushing down the river, captured a series of important places including Song, Kapit, Kanowit and eventually Sibu, the second largest town in Sarawak. Fisher's work was particularly valuable in dealing with the Ibans whose violent tempers and passions were more easily roused than those of the Kenyahs, Kayans, Kelabits and other inland people to the south and east.

Semut II relied largely on the Kenyahs who were under the excellent control of their paramount chief, Tama Weng Ajang. Courtney and Harrisson flew over to him at Long Akar on the Baram after visiting Sochon and so tied up matters which would have taken weeks by signal. The main concern of all the Semut leaders was the movement of Japanese escapees from Brunei towards Ukong on the Limbang River. They were mainly from Miri and the Lutong oilfields, and Carter, who had earlier taken Marudi, had been forced back by this group. They had then, despite vigorous resistance from the Kenyahs, pushed their way into the Tutoh and headed up river to the north-east. Their numbers were said to be between 1,500 and 2,000 and the possibility that this large, hungry, well-armed and disciplined force might get in among the very vulnerable long houses along the river banks was alarming. It was decided that the Japanese must be opposed all the way, picked off, given no rest, led astray and worn down. But the effort was mounted too late and involved ex-SOE officers unfamiliar with Borneo jungle, so that a first-class mess was created which led to vituperative exchanges between the Semut commanders, during which time the Japanese column passed out of the Semut II area and became the responsibility of Semut I until after the end of the war.

It now became a matter of deep concern to find out what the Japanese, pressing inland, were trying to do. Reports from Edmeades, east of the Crocker ranges, and from Blondeel in Dutch Borneo showed that the Japanese from both coasts were moving in a northerly direction. Harrisson realized that the first thing to do was to screen all approaches and he sent Lieutenant Westley down to Long Nawan with a party of Kenyahs which included Along, the son of the great chief. This completed the screening, for he was shielded by Semut II and III to the west and east and could pay particular attention to the Japanese columns moving northwards. At this point Z Special Headquarters sent in to Harrisson an adjutant in the shape of Captain P. Bartram, whose very tall, shy, thoroughly indoor, Oxford-donnish appearance hid a very effective and efficient mind. He was able to relieve Harrisson of much of his paperwork and this enabled him to move about more among his eccentric subordinates whose actions and reactions at times, although with the best of intentions, had been somewhat too individual.

In the east and north-east the Japanese were moving

along the Sembakong River towards Pensiagan, a small town just inside the North Borneo border, and since neither Semut nor Agas to the north had any effective guerrillas in the area, there was nothing to prevent the Japanese column moving on. But Blondeel organized his forces to attack at night by ambushes, while the RAAF co-operated by day by picking off targets along the Sembakong River. Blondeel was fortunate in having under his theoretical control a large group of Sea Dayaks who for some years had been on one of their periodical hunting and jungle foraging expeditions, although their homes were hundreds of miles to the south. The Sea Dayaks employed a frontal method of attack and this, together with their jungle craft and the use of surprise, earned them many heads.

The Japanese never adapted to movement in the jungle – they went fully equipped and could be heard, smelt and seen long before they came within striking distance. They had no chance against a people who had been hunting game and each other for generations and particularly against the soundless blow pipe and poisoned dart.

The only way the Japanese could hope to fight successfully was to stay, as far as possible, in force and in open spaces, of which there were very few in the jungle. It soon became clear that all their commands were heading for a final stand in an area where their firepower and massed tactics would pay off. That was why Pensiagan, which was one of the few places having lines of supply and retreat not completely cut off by Semut, was being built up as a staging post with machine-gun posts, air-raid shelters and other defence works. From Pensiagan the Japanese columns began to trickle towards the Sapong estate which lay at the head of the single North Borneo railway line. This estate was one of the biggest in Borneo and provided much in the way of space and other amenities. Its value as a defensive area was greatly enhanced because it could only be approached through the narrow and very deep Padas Gorge.

Harrisson felt that now was the time for the Australian Army to help him, but they were much less co-operative than the RAAF whose Beaufighters he steered in on their first shoot up. The Australian Army felt that the Japanese were finished anyhow and were reluctant to risk lives. They took a great deal of persuading that Sapong was becoming a concentration area and that there were already some 2,000 Japanese troops there. Harrisson, realizing that any help he was going to receive from the regular army would be slow in coming, if it came at all, put into effect the Semut plan for dealing with the situation.

The Japanese had housed their men in huts in the high cane grass, presumably to avoid spotting from aircraft, but this rendered them very susceptible to fire. So, with the co-operation of the RAAF, it was proposed to set light to the high grass and then deal with the Japanese by steadily increasing guerrilla attacks by the Tagals, aided in a wider circuit by the Kelabits, Muruts and Chinese. Meanwhile Edmeades deployed 200 men on the east side of the Crocker Range around the headwaters of the Mengalong in the Iburu–Bole sector. These areas had sites suitable for dropping supplies and reinforcements and would prove very handy for launching the harassing and wearing attacks at which the guerrillas were becoming very adept.

The Japanese columns moving slowly towards Sapong were harried all the way up the Tengoa valley and when they eventually staggered out into the open they were immediately attacked by the waiting guerrillas. It was conservatively estimated that at least 400 were killed, quite apart from the suicides which began to occur during the march, and some involuntary suicides brought about when hungry Japanese ate raw, unhusked padi which swelled up and burst their stomachs.

Of that time Edmeades records:

The fight went on all the way through the Ulu Tomani and Tomani down past Kemabong into the Sapong estate itself. Ricter and I left MacPherson and Griffiths at Bole and with Bower and a party of guerrilla soldiers we carried out a follow-up operation, picking off stragglers and generally making a nuisance of ourselves wherever possible. We followed the remnants of the Japanese column right into Sapong estate where all remaining enemy forces were being regrouped at this stage. Presumably the Japanese intended their last-ditch stand to be carried out there and their strength was reported as being between three and four thousand at the time. I next sent Sergeant Hayes with a wireless set to report more closely on Japanese movements and the patrolling of the Sapong area. This he carried out most successfully, sitting almost on top of General Baba's headquarters for nearly three weeks, with little food and often surrounded by Japanese.

There was now a Japanese column debouching from the coast into the upper reaches of the Limbang River fifty miles to the west and it was faced with a walk into Sapong which had never been done in human knowledge. The column would have to travel right up the Limbang to avoid the 6,000 ft terrain in the ranges of Pagan Priok. There were no river craft available (the guerrillas had seen to that) and there were no crops or people in the forest and river valley. The march would take at least fifteen days and this would give time for Harrisson to resite his large and excellent forces in Trusan to meet the Japanese after their overland crossing of the Limbang watershed south of the Pagan Priok massif. The Japanese would then have another 100-mile march over extremely difficult country every mile of which was known to the guerrilla forces. Their casualties would be very heavy.

At this point, when everything was poised for action, came the order to all guerrilla and other forces in Borneo to cease operations against the Japanese. Two atomic bombs had been dropped on Japan and the Japanese had surrendered.

This sudden end to the all-absorbing, bitterly fought war inside Borneo was a tremendous shock to those concerned. They had been living in a state of nervous tension, their whole purpose being the destruction of the enemy, and the sudden ending at first left a feeling of emptiness, only partly filled when, inevitably, the administrative machine, both in the forces and the government, began the herculean task of undoing what had been done, a process that would take years. But for Harrisson and several of the others the war was not quite over. Major-General Wootten, commanding the Australian 9th Division, still chose not to believe that there were strong Japanese forces at Sapong and would not help other than by taking the credit for all that the Semut parties had done, but Harrisson, subtly and strongly backed by Z headquarters, was doing his best to make sure that the people of the interior who had to be disarmed would not be left to the mercies of the Japanese columns still winding their way towards Sapong. Fortunately Major-General Wootten was replaced by Brigadier Windeyer who was able to believe the evidence of his eyes and realized that something must be done. He allowed Harrisson to ask for volunteers from the Z personnel already withdrawn from the field and the latter was most fortunate to get Major R. Blow who had been in Agas with Combe and Chester.

Harrisson and Blow set off for the wide Trusan valley where the main body of Japanese en route to Sapong were congregating and where there would be fighting unless an order from Major-General Baba ordering the Japanese there to surrender could be got to them rapidly. Harrisson

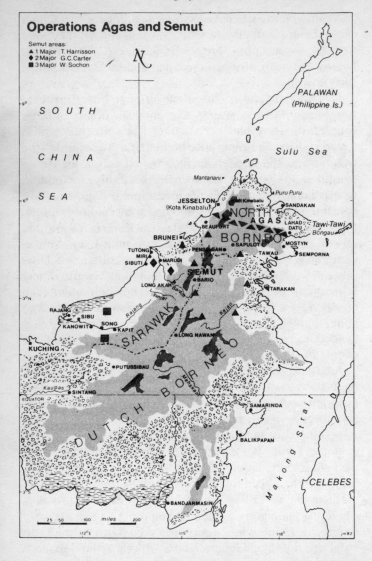

Operations Agas and Semut

Semut areas:
▲ 1 Major T. Harrisson
♦ 2 Major G.C. Carter
■ 3 Major W. Sochon

N

SOUTH

CHINA

SEA

9°

6°

3°N

EQUATOR

3°S

PALAWAN
(Philippine Is.)

Sulu Sea

Mantanani •

• Puru Puru

• Mt Kinabalu
JESSELTON
(Kota Kinabalu)

NORTH

AGAS

BORNEO

• SANDAKAN

BEAUFORT •

LAHAD
DATU
Tawi-Tawi
Bengau

BRUNEI

PENSIANGAN

• SAPULOT

MOSTYN

TUTONG
MIRI
SIBUTI

MARUDI

SEMUT

• TAWAU

SEMPORNA

LONG AKAH

• BARIO

• TARAKAN

RAJANG
SIBU
KANOWIT

SONG

KAPIT

SARAWAK

Rajang

Baram

Tinjar

Kajan

BORNEO

• LONG NAWAN

KUCHING

• PUTUSSIBAU

Kapuas

DUTCH

Kapuas

SAMARINDA

Kaupas
SINTANG

Barito

BALIKPAPAN

Makong Strait

CELEBES

• BANDJARMASIN

25 50   100   miles   200
112°E   115°   118°   jm 82

also had with him a Japanese officer and a young signals officer from the 9th Division. As they moved off they were greeted enthusiastically by their tried and trusted Murut–Kelabit guerrillas and such leaders as Yita Singh, the Dayak leader Usop and others. As Harrisson and his group were supposed to have no arms it was difficult to keep the 9th Division Headquarters informed of their *peaceful* progress.

The Japanese had emerged from the Trusan on to a wide, fertile and irrigated plain at the foot of Mount Murud and there they were set upon by several hundred of the Bawang troops and for the next two days there was haphazard fighting all over the plain and around its edges. Finally Harrisson arrived with the Japanese officer, the signals officer and the radio to find that the Japanese had withdrawn to a position on a knoll in the centre of the plain. Equipped with a vast white flag the Japanese officer went across to the Japanese camp and presently emerged accompanied by the Japanese commanding officer who handed Harrisson his sword as he stood beside a rice hut. It was 30 October, 1945, and later that afternoon the formal surrender of the Japanese was accepted. Once again the fire started by a few courageous and determined men had taken hold among the peoples of Borneo and made it impossible for the Japanese ever to subdue them, let alone to conquer them in the name of their much vaunted Co-Prosperity Sphere.

6
Rimau

While the planning for Agas and Semut had been going on at Services Reconnaissance Department Headquarters in Melbourne, South-East Asia Command, now convinced of the feasibility of long-range attacks on shipping by other than conventional means, was actively considering a dual attack against Japanese shipping under the codename of 'Hornbill'.

One attack was to be against the Japanese-occupied port of Saigon, then part of French Indo-China, the other was originally to be on Batavia, but Lyon, who was to lead the attack, had a fanatical determination to return to Singapore, and, despite all the solid arguments against attacking the same port twice, those in command in Melbourne allowed themselves to be persuaded that another such attack was feasible.

However, they cannot have examined very carefully the all-important details on which the success or failure of the operation depended, and the lives of the men who undertook it. It is significant that both Davidson and Page were suspicious of the operation, which was codenamed 'Rimau' (the Malay word for tiger), from the start and only went because of their great regard for Lyon, voicing the thought that he was crazy but that they could not let him down.

In addition to Lyon there went from the Jaywick team Davidson, Page, Falls, Huston and Marsh. Sixteen other officers and men were recruited from the British and Australian Armies, from the Royal Marines, the Royal Australian Navy and the Royal Naval Volunteer Reserve.

The party was to be transported by the British mine-laying submarine *Porpoise* (Lieutenant-Commander Marchant RN) which had been specially converted for their use.

The plan, in its bare essentials, was for the *Porpoise* to take them to the target area and there they would locate and capture a junk from which they proposed to operate. This was the first big difference between Jaywick and Rimau – the capture of the junk; and immediately it raised some very difficult points. First of all, were they going to find a suitable junk in the right place at the right time? Secondly, could they capture it without raising an alarm? Thirdly, would not the junk be missed? Fourthly, could they sail it into position without arousing interest?

But the crux of the matter was that they proposed to use a new type of submersible attack craft. This had the official title of Motor Submersible Canoe and was a twelve-foot-long, metal, canoe-shaped boat with diving planes and ballast tanks. It was driven by an electric motor from heavy electric batteries, but a point of great weakness in the design was that the batteries had to be vented by a small nozzle on the foredeck which was closed by a rubber band. If this was absent or damaged the battery compartment filled with water and the 'Sleeping Beauty', as the canoe was codenamed, sank like a stone and the operator, who was wearing watertight clothing and oxygen breathing apparatus which left no trace of bubbles on the surface, had to get out of the open cockpit in a hurry and swim to the surface where his chance of survival was very small indeed, what with the Japanese above and the sharks below.

The Sleeping Beauty had two speeds, full ahead and half-speed, and in still water its maximum speed would be about four knots. How it was supposed to cope with the tides off Singapore, which can run at over six knots, had been left to fate. Steering and elevation was by means of an aircraft type 'joy stick' and on a panel in front of the operator was a compass which was usually highly inaccurate, affected as it was by the electrical circuits in the metal hull.

As attack craft the Sleeping Beauties carried their limpets on the foredeck and immediately there came the problem of one man handling the difficult trim of his submersible at the same time as trying to fix cordtex-linked limpets below water on hulls which might be rusty. He would need to have the craft held against the bilge by positive buoyancy, which meant altering the trim and taking vital minutes to re-alter it when leaving the target.

Before an attack the operator had to adjust his trim to slightly negative buoyancy and approach his target, submerged, by a series of porpoise-like underwater swoops, which allowed his head to emerge briefly and gave him a chance to get his direction. This could be done reasonably well in smooth water if the particular Sleeping Beauty was performing normally, but at night and in rough water it would be extremely difficult to reach a target, for endurance was limited and the batteries could only be recharged out of water, which meant several men to move them. This required either a safe shore base or a secure mother ship and the idea of a pirated junk being used for this purpose was absurd in the extreme.

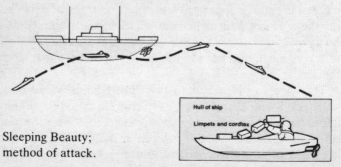

Sleeping Beauty;
method of attack.

Lyon had in mind the agonizing hours of paddling in Folboats on the Jaywick operation when he opted for the Sleeping Beauties, but I do not believe he had ever thought out, let alone practised, a full-scale operation in difficult conditions. The so-called rehearsals at Garden Island went to show how unreliable these craft were and how very difficult it would be to keep them in good order, especially under the stress of operations, but it would seem that Lyon's drive and fanaticism overcame or blinded to realities those responsible for approving the attack, and on 11 September, 1944, the *Porpoise* left Careening Bay on Garden Island.

In addition to the crew and the raiding party and conducting officers, the *Porpoise* carried in her already cramped accommodation fifteen Sleeping Beauties, painted black, eleven Folboats, arms, ammunition, grenades, limpets, radios and fifteen tons of food and other supplies. It could not have helped the mental or physical condition of the party to be so accommodated and there was little chance for them to get fresh air or to exercise.

The *Porpoise* cut through Lombok Strait at night, running at fifteen knots on the surface, then submerged at dawn north of Bali and travelled through the Carimata Strait between Borneo and Billiton by daylight, surfacing at night to cross the China Sea.

On the afternoon of 23 September she reached Merapas Island which is the most easterly island of the Rhio Archipelago and which Lyon had selected as a rear base. Lieutenant-Commander Marchant, who knew that he was only sixty miles from the Japanese seaplane base on Chempa Island, had kept the *Porpoise* submerged all day, despite the dangerously shallow water. At less than twenty fathoms he made a periscope reconnaissance of the island. It seemed to be uninhabited and at dusk the *Porpoise* surfaced 400 yards from a beach and Davidson and Corporal Stewart went ashore in a Folboat to check. They returned in three hours to report that, although there were some old footmarks in the jungle, the island was uninhabited and that there was a spring.

It was then too late to land stores so the *Porpoise* moved into deeper water and submerged, returning the next evening. A periscope sweep showed three Malays on the beach but Lyon and Davidson thought that they were stray visitors from another island and that the decision to make Merapas Base A for Rimau should stand. However, the presence of Malays made it essential to guard the stores which were to have been buried and left; so they were put ashore in charge of Lieutenant Carey, the No 2 Conducting Officer and a commando, and incidentally the brother of the Carey who had led the Scorpion raid.

The next step was to pirate a junk and the *Porpoise* left Merapas, submerged, early on 25 September, making for Pejantan Island which was about 140 miles away between the Rhio Archipelago and Borneo. Pejantan was reached on 26 September and a periscope reconnaissance and subsequent exploration showed that it was uninhabited and ideal as a rallying and pick-up point. Then the *Porpoise* went searching for a suitable craft to capture and at 4 P.M. on 28 September near a small island named Datuk, about thirty miles off Pontianak, she found the *Mustika*, a Canton-type junk of about 100 tons making from Borneo to Rhio along the traditional junk route. The *Porpoise* closed and surfaced beside the junk and Lyon and Davidson led seven armed men aboard while others covered them from the submarine. The Malay captain and his crew of eight were so astonished that they did not attempt to fight but protested strongly when made to sail the junk back towards Pejantan Island. The *Porpoise* had slipped astern and submerged, surfacing at dusk to take the junk in tow for the night and submerging again next morning. There was a steady breeze and the junk, making six knots, reached the island during the afternoon of 29 September, anchoring off a beach on the northern coast.

The *Porpoise* came alongside at dusk and all that night the Rimau party and the crew worked at transferring the Sleeping Beauties and the stores to the junk but, by dawn, the transfer had not been completed so the *Porpoise* submerged for the day, returning the same evening to complete unloading.

Early on 1 October the Malay crew of the *Mustika* were transferred to the *Porpoise* under the care of Major Chapman, the Senior Conducting Officer, and at 3 A.M. she sailed for Australia, arriving at Fremantle on 11 October.

What happened to Operation Rimau after the *Porpoise* left is known accurately only in part, owing to lack of evidence and the Official Secrets Act. Suffice it to say that the role played by the submarine due to pick up the Rimau party from Merapas was so extraordinary that it can only have been due to a misunderstanding of the plan, which was in itself a poor one. The pick-up submarine was not the *Porpoise* but another one on operational patrol, whose primary duty was to attack enemy shipping. She embarked Major Chapman and Corporal Croton on 15 October, 1944, and left on patrol. She was due to pick up the Rimau party on 8 November and, *if that rendezvous was not kept, the party was to wait up to a further thirty days and, if not picked up by then, they were to make their own way home*. How they were to do this was never stated.

As a piece of planning the concept was woeful. In the type of operations undertaken by Services Reconnaissance Department it was essential to keep *the first rendezvous*. Lyon, Davidson and Page must have known the extreme danger of trying to keep hidden for perhaps thirty days in an archipelago which could easily be searched by the huge numbers of troops available to the Japanese. Why they agreed to the proposal is beyond comprehension.

On 7 November the submarine still had on board fifteen torpedoes and sufficient fuel and stores for another fifteen days' patrolling, and her commander was loath to leave his patrol to pick up the Rimau party on the 8th. So, with the concurrence of Major Chapman, he postponed the first pick-up until 21 November. On that day the submarine reconnoitred Merapas by periscope and spent the day submerged at sea, returning at 1 A.M. on the 22nd when Major Chapman and Corporal Croton were dropped 500 yards offshore and paddled in by Folboat. The submarine then put to sea and submerged until the following day when it returned at 9.30 P.M. and surfaced off the northwest corner of Merapas. Soon after, Major Chapman and Corporal Croton returned aboard and reported no sign of the party, although there were signs that they had been there some fourteen days before. No messages had been left and there was no evidence of a struggle.

It was then agreed that nothing further would be gained by remaining in the area and trying again at a later date and the submarine then left for Fremantle. *The incredible fact is that, despite orders, there was no attempt made to keep the second rendezvous whose last day was 8 December, and that if the first date had been kept the party would probably have been picked up. No explanation of this has ever been given.*

It is probable that the *Mustika* sailed from Pejantan on 1 October and called at Merapas where four men were left to help Lieutenant Carey. At this time the raiding party would have adopted the disguises used in the Jaywick operation, i.e. dark body stain and sarongs when on deck, and the junk would have been flying the 'Poached Egg' flag and the Japanese Military Government flag. After leaving Merapas the *Mustika* sailed due south to the Temiang Strait up which she hurried and continued through the Sugi Strait. On 6 October she was off Laban Island, about ten miles south-east of Keppel Harbour and there Lyon decided to anchor and wait for dark before launching the Sleeping Beauty attack. But, while they were preparing their craft, a Malay inspector, from the water police control point on Kasu Island three miles away, set out in a police patrol launch to check up on the *Mustika*. His name was Bin Shiapel and he had with him two Malay constables. When the party on the *Mustika* saw the launch they must have assumed it was Japanese and went to action stations. Then someone on board made a mistake and, instead of capturing the crew of the launch without using firearms, opened fire with a silenced Sten gun. There and then Operation Rimau was wrecked. Somehow one Malay constable reached Laban Island and gave the alarm.

Lyon decided that the only thing to do was to blow the *Mustika* with its secret Sleeping Beauties and retreat as fast as possible. They sailed in the dark down Phillip Channel and when some sixteen miles from Singapore, off the island of Kapala Jernih west of Bulan Island, the *Mustika* was sunk and, in four parties led by Lyon, Davidson, Page and Ross, the Folboats started their long and desperate paddle back to Merapas Island to keep the rendezvous on 8 November, four weeks and five days ahead.

The first reaction of the 7th Area Army Command who controlled Singapore was one almost of indifference. It was not until Captain Tomita, commanding a search party of one company of men, was killed on Mapor Island, just near Merapas, that the Army Command was roused and Major Koshida, an experienced officer with a fully

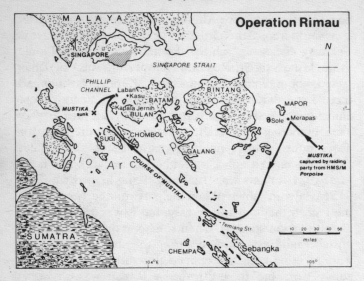

equipped battalion of well-trained troops, was sent to search the thousand islands and told not to return until he had killed or captured the enemy.

Evidence seems to show that all four parties met on Sole Island near Merapas and there clashed with the Japanese, during which Lyon and Ross were killed; then it seems that the rest dispersed to other islands to await the pick-up on 8 November. During this time Davidson and Huston were killed between the islands of Sole and Mapor. In the end, after two months' search, Major Koshida and his battalion killed ten men and captured ten out of the total Rimau force of twenty-three.

Three men led by Lieutenant Sargent (the names of the other two are not known) broke through the Japanese cordon in their Folboat and then began an escape saga which, if it had succeeded, would most surely have taken its place in history. The three paddled by night for more than two months, somehow evading capture and getting food, for nearly two thousand miles, always moving eastwards from the Rhio Archipelago along the edges of Sumatra and Java, Bali and Lombok, Sumbawa, Flores, Alor, Wetar, to the Romang Islands north-east of Timor only some 400 miles from Darwin. There the two un-named men met their end, one believed to have been taken by sharks and the other killed by a Chinese when the Folboat was wrecked. Lieutenant Sargent was captured in an extreme state of exhaustion, extremely thin and malaria ridden.

The eleven prisoners were taken to Singapore. They were Major R. N. Ingleton, Captain R. C. Page, Lieutenant W. G. Carey, Warrant Officer A. Warren, Sergeant D. P. Gooley, Corporal C. M. Stewart, Corporal R. B. Fletcher, Lance-Corporal J. T. Hardy, Able Seaman Falls, Able Seaman Marsh and Lieutenant Sargent. Of these Able Seaman Marsh died of malaria on Christmas Day, 1944.

The Japanese regarded their captives as heroes, but that did not prevent them putting them on trial, and eventually beheading them, which, in the Japanese tradition, is the proper ending for brave men and a mark of great respect. The executions took place on 7 July, 1945.

So ended Operation Rimau.

7

Timor

Rimau had taken place while preparations were being made for Agas and Semut but in 1942, before any of these actions had been considered, a small group, an offshoot of Z Special Force, had been operating on Timor, an island to the north of Australia, alongside an Allied Force, which consisted originally of Australian and Dutch troops.

The Japanese occupied the island in great strength but, after their initial success, they were held down in an almost unbelievably successful campaign by units of the Australian Independent Company, while the Z Special group functioned as a subversive and intelligence-gathering unit. In February, 1943, after the final withdrawal of the Independent Company, a number of Z Special groups, operating from Lugger Maintenance Section in Darwin, were left on Timor until the surrender of the Japanese.

Timor is less than 600 miles from Darwin and is about 227 miles long and some 62 miles wide, with a very precipitous mountain chain down its centre. Before the Second World War the west end of the island was controlled by the Dutch and the east end by the Portuguese; there were also some Portuguese enclaves in the Dutch area.

The indigenous people are of the Indonesian–Malay type, liberally interlaced with the progeny of the many other people who have, from time to time, invaded the island or come there to trade: the Portuguese, the Dutch, Chinese, Indians, etc. They were all kept under control by the Dutch and Portuguese, using a small number of troops and local police forces.

In Australia it was appreciated that any attack on Australia itself might well use Timor as a springboard and for this reason there was an agreement with the Dutch, made in January, 1941, that help would be sent to Timor and to Ambon, off the island of Seram, if war with Japan broke out. However, when Japan attacked Pearl Harbor in December, 1941, there were three Australian divisions fighting in the Middle East and one division, less one brigade, in Malaya. From this brigade of the 8th Division one battalion had been sent to Rabaul in New Britain early in 1941, while the remainder of the brigade was held in Darwin. These very small forces were all that Australia could produce locally, bearing in mind a population of only seven million and the overseas divisions.

War was declared on the Japanese after the attack on Pearl Harbour and on 12 December, 1941, the 2/21st and the 2/40th Battalions went to Timor and Ambon as arranged. The 2/4th Pioneer Battalion also set out for Timor but was turned back by Japanese attack. In addition there went small numbers of units such as anti-tank gunners, heavy gunners to man the coastal defences, signallers, anti-aircraft gunners and a specialized force of the Australian Army known as the 2/2nd Independent Company.

Although Services Reconnaissance Department in several guises was involved in the Timor campaign it was the 2/2nd Independent Company, together with a sister unit, which was basically responsible for the ridiculously understated and quite phenomenal achievement of immobilizing a reinforced Japanese division of 15,000 experienced men who had fought in China, Java and the Philippines. No praise is sufficient for the magnificent fight they put up between 1941 and 1943 over the length and breadth of Timor.

The men, who were all volunteers, had already been

trained to normal Army standards and were drawn mostly from country districts. Ninety per cent were from Western Australia and accustomed to hard physical work in an arid, harsh climate. They were skilled at making themselves comfortable under difficult conditions and as they found the greater part of Timor to be covered in thin, forest scrub on stony hills, the terrain was quite familiar to most of them.

At No 7 Infantry Training Centre on Wilson's Promontory the men went through the commando course, which called for very high standards of physical fitness and intelligence. Each company had on its strength an engineer officer, a signals officer and a medical officer. Officers and non-commissioned officers were trained in the new methods for six weeks and then the independent companies were formed by allocating the trained officers to units created from normally trained men. The newly created companies were then put through a further six weeks of intensive training and made ready for operations.

Initially four companies were fashioned in this manner. The 2/1st Company operated in the islands north-east of Australia from Manus to the New Hebrides. The 2/3rd was sent to New Caledonia and the 2/2nd to Timor, where they were relieved by the 2/4th. The 2/2nd were moved to Timor on the *Zealandia*, a troopship used in the war of 1914-18, and landed at Koepang in west Timor. It was a small port with inadequate facilities for the 2,000 troops assembled there. Apart from the Australians there were 230 Dutch troops under Colonel Dettinger and he told Colonel W. W. Leggatt, DSO, MC, the commander of the combined group known as 'Sparrow Force', that, in Portuguese Timor to the east, their army consisted of some 500 officers, non-commissioned officers and other ranks armed with four, possibly six, Vickers heavy machine-guns and some Winchester rifles which were at least forty years old. The troops were Timorese, officered by Portuguese.

Portugal had never declared war on Japan, and never did, and the problem of their attitude to Sparrow Force was the subject of much hasty diplomatic interchange, which resulted in the Portuguese government in Lisbon ordering an increase in their garrison strength on Timor by 5,000 soldiers to be sent from Mozambique, 6,000 miles away. These troops had reached the half-way point in their voyage to Timor by the time that the Japanese gained control of the sea in that area and they refused a safe conduct for the ship carrying the troops, so it turned back to Africa.

Eventually, and rather grudgingly, the governor of Portuguese Timor agreed to its occupation by Dutch troops from Sparrow Force, assisted by the 2/2nd Independent Company. Sparrow Force itself was not in good condition. Only Colonel Leggatt and two of the sergeants had ever been in action before and that had been in the First World War. Over fifty men had never fired a rifle and the equipment and clothing of the force left much to be desired. In Koepang the men contracted malaria and dysentery and inevitably morale was affected by the non-arrival of reinforcements due to Japanese bombing of transports at sea.

By a stroke of good fortune Mr Ross, an Australian who was the British Consul in Dili in Portuguese Timor, had arrived in Koepang on a visit and proved to be a great help at all times. Tall, lean and with a pronounced sense of humour, he filled in the background of the country and its customs for them all and later paved the way for their reception in Dili by the Portuguese governor, Manuel d'Abreu Ferreira de Carvalho.

The Independent Company moved out to Dili aerodrome and disposed troops around it, at the same time arranging fields of fire and booby traps. The Dutch contingent occupied a building on the waterfront towards the east end of the town. The occupation took place on 17 December, 1941, and was hailed in faraway newspapers as the first act of realism and offensive action carried out by the Allies in the Second World War.

There followed a period of intense activity for the Independent Company and at first they were hampered by poor communications, heavy rains and malaria. One disturbing feature of this disease was the very slow rate of recovery and in most cases a man was still in a very weak state three weeks after the attack. Gradually the health of the men improved, but the weeks of malaria incurred during January, 1942, left their mark. However, the mobility of the men was greatly helped by the fact that each acquired a Timorese servant called in the local dialect a 'criado'. These boys or men would relieve the soldiers of their packs and other heavy belongings and go off into the bush with them during action so that the troops could concentrate on their fighting. Afterwards they would be guided to safety by the criados.

As the troops became more familiar with the country the help the criados gave became more and more useful. The north coast near Dili has a narrow coastal plain with ridges rising steeply from it; behind them the mountains rose tier on tier to the 10,000 ft central massifs of Ramelau and Cablac. The rivers had cut steep and tortuous gorges through the mountains and the whole was made more complicated by spurs and razor-backed ridges which had been thrown up by earlier geological action. Once over the mountains to the south the scene changed somewhat, as the ridges were longer and more gradual and there were plains running back between them sometimes ten miles or more in width behind the coastal belt of swamp. To the west, near the Dutch border, the wide Nunura Plains extended from behind Mallana north to the mouth of the River Lois. To the east the hills, though extremely steep, dropped in height to some five or six thousand feet in the Mundo-Perdido range before falling abruptly to a small coastal plain running to the north-east end of the island.

The road system was meagre and, though well-graded, it was blocked from time to time by landslides, but the Portuguese 'postos' (administrative centres) were also linked by a complex system of routes capable of use by the sure-footed Timorese horses, and the soldiers made a point of getting to know them, as well as the location of villages and gardens.

Radio communication was difficult because of the very broken nature of the country which foiled the low power of the Company's sets, never built for more than short distance linking. There was no news of approaching Japanese forces but the radio told of their advances through Malaya and the Philippines and of the fall of Singapore. Neither the forces round Koepang nor the smaller forces in and around Dili had any means of knowing the overall strategy of the Allies, but a total of some 700 troops was scarcely sufficient to hold a colony containing a population of more than 600,000 people.

The night of 19 February, like most other nights in Dili, was close, humid and hot. There was a fair amount of fog hanging about offshore and, if there were any lookouts posted, they could not see anything. Captain Callinan and his brother officers had eaten a late supper with the Dutch officers and gone to bed about half past ten when their sleep was rudely shattered by shells whistling in from the sea, the first of which hit the barracks and killed several people.

The troops hastily took to their trenches, which had been dug outside the barracks, while the enemy craft offshore illuminated the target with a searchlight and then

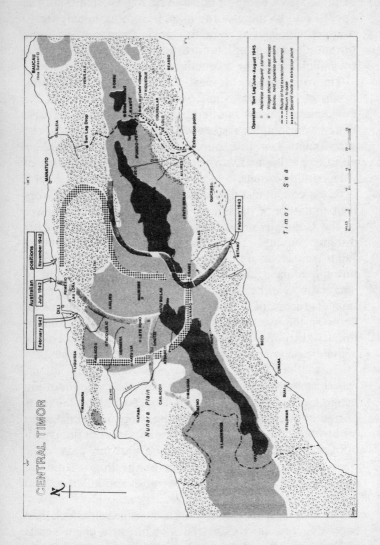

fired. Colonel van Straten thought at first that it was an enemy submarine but it soon became evident that a landing was in progress. Captain Callinan ordered Lieutenant Mackenzie's platoon to send out a patrol to investigate lights coming from the direction of the Comoro River to the west of Dili. Soon after, Private Doyle reported to Captain Callinan from Mackenzie that the Japanese had come marching up the road towards Dili in threes and had been mown down at short range by Private Ryan on the Bren gun until his number two on the gun had been killed by a grenade. Mackenzie and his men were holding off Japanese efforts to take the aerodrome by well-directed fire from positions that had been prepared long before.

Dawn found Colonel van Straten, Callinan and Doyle moving back to a new headquarters in the hills behind the town and from the high ground the enemy transports and warships could be seen keeping discreetly out of range since one of their destroyers had been hit twice by Captain de Winter's ancient artillery. Mackenzie and his section, using bayonets, had kept the Japanese off the aerodrome, while Sapper Richards crouched in a slit trench with his hand on the exploder which would blow the aerodrome.

At dawn Mackenzie realized he could not hold his position any longer and gave orders to withdraw and blow the aerodrome. The sappers had arranged three alternative methods of firing, so, despite the earlier attentions of a fifth columnist – he had been caught cutting connecting wires and had been shot – the demolition was a great success. So much so that Corporal Curran, retiring at speed, suddenly found the ground opening before him as a crater formed. Curran, later promoted Lieutenant, was forced to conceal himself all day in short grass with a myopic Japanese sentry perched on a knoll above him. At dusk he crawled out of his hiding place and two days later rejoined his company, the burns from the hot stones on which he had lain still raw on his chest.

All patrols now moved back rapidly to company head-quarters at Cailaco and preparations were made for the beginning of sustained guerrilla warfare. At the same time as the Japanese had landed approximately 1,000 troops at Dili, they had landed 5,000 in the vicinity of Koepang, with further waves following closely. These troops were veterans and included a regiment of the 38th Division, which had been instrumental in capturing Hong Kong, 630 paratroops put down in two drops, a detachment of marines and a section of light tanks. Against such odds there was little that Sparrow Force could do, but, under Colonel Leggatt, they fought a determined rearguard action, moving to the east to have more room to man-oeuvre. The Japanese paratroops functioned chiefly as snipers and adopted a favourite tactic in climbing coconut palms and tying themselves there while continuing to snipe at the enemy until they themselves were shot dead. Of the 630 paratroops only seventy-eight survived, but they effectively slowed down the movement of Sparrow Force until, after four days of continuous fighting, Japanese tanks had caught up and encircled the force and the Japanese commander asked for a parley.

Colonel Leggatt, who found it difficult to keep his officers awake, so great was their exhaustion, sent his interpreter to speak with the Japanese commander. When he returned Colonel Leggatt asked him what the Japanese commander had said.

'He says he wants to surrender,' said the interpreter. Colonel Leggatt laughed. Japanese is a difficult language.

'You go back and ask him again,' he said.

So Sparrow Force, except for a few Dutch and Austra-lian troops who escaped, surrendered to the enemy on 23

February and army headquarters in Australia, hearing the news, assumed that this included the Independent Company as well. Communications between Koepang and Dili had broken down so that neither the Independent Company nor the Dutch knew of the surrender. They had decided to establish hidden reserves of ammunition and food to serve as bases to which attacking patrols could retire and in general they arranged to attack the enemy wherever and whenever possible, but they needed relatively secure areas in which men returning from operations could rest. There was also the necessity to establish a safe area for Captain Dunkley, the Medical Officer, to set up a hospital. In view of all this the headquarters was moved back across the Glano River.

The attitude of the Timorese was of the greatest importance, for it is an axiom of guerrilla warfare that it will only succeed if the population is on the side of the guerrillas. In Dutch Timor the people had very quickly gone over to the Japanese and had betrayed and murdered many Allied troops. So far, in Portuguese Timor, they had stood resolutely by the Allies, because in Dutch Timor the population had seen that the Dutch were not successful against the Japanese, whereas in Portuguese Timor the Australians and Dutch had already demonstrated their competence and success. The Timorese were realists and could see no future in assisting Europeans who were being defeated. Later, towards the end of the campaign in Eastern Timor, when the Australians were exhausted and greatly outnumbered, the Timorese turned against them for the same reason. For the moment, however, the local Timorese were pro-European and in this attitude they were influenced also by the fact that the Roman Catholic Church had established missions throughout the eastern half of Timor and the priests and nuns had considerable sway over their flocks.

Because there was no communication with Koepang, and in view of the many wild rumours flying about, Captain Callinan decided to see for himself what was happening to the west. He went down as far as Hatu Lia on the only motor-cycle left and there met Lieutenant Horstink of the Royal Netherlands East India Army who had been one of the last to leave Dili and had brought 100 men with him. Callinan then picked up some horses and men and reached Cailaco after dark where Lieutenant Burridge reported no Japanese nearby. Next morning he crossed the River Lois, the Dutch/Portuguese frontier, and after walking across the dry, hot coralline country until five in the afternoon they came to the Catholic Mission at Lahoeroes. They were welcomed most hospitably and heard, for the first time, the news of the fall of Koepang and of the arrival of an Australian brigadier on the island to take over command. Some looting of Chinese shops had been going on in Lahoeroes and Callinan and his men put a stop to it. Then a Captain Parker with seven Australian troops came in. Next morning the return journey began and the enlarged party reached their headquarters two days later, meeting Major Spence en route to contact the Brigadier who was on the south coast.

When looked at in cold blood the situation was now little short of appalling. Opposed to the overwhelming strength of the Japanese, there were the Independent Company and a few troops from units which had surrendered in Koepang. However, the Australians had the advantage of extreme mobility, a co-operative population and sufficient food supplies, and it was on these premises that the bases from which to operate their guerrilla war were organized. In general the bases ran from Memo on the Dutch-Portuguese border through Maliana (Lieutenant Rose) to Cailaco (Lieutenant Dexter), from there to Rotai (Lieutenant Turton) and then up to Hatu Builau

under the high mountain Tata Mailau (9,000 ft) where
Lieutenant Mackenzie held watch and ward; north from
there to Lieutenant Boyland near Ailieu and then down to
Lieutenant Laidlaw near Remexio from which the road
running along the north coast could be observed and
ambushed.

This line made use of the central massif and backed on
to the escape routes to the south coast. It also included
Company Headquarters at Bobonaro, the hospital at
Ainaro and Force Headquarters at Mape in which Brigadier Veale was established. It was he who had landed at
Koepang a few days before it surrendered and had taken
control of the Australian troops who had escaped the
surrender.

Soon after Captain Callinan had returned from his
abortive foray to Koepang a message reached him from
the British Consul, Mr Ross, that the Japanese had sent
him to negotiate a surrender of the remaining forces and
would Captain Callinan please contact him. The meeting
took place at Hatu Lia and Ross was amazed and pleased
to find the Australians in high spirits with a reasonable
amount of food. The proposals put forward by the
Japanese were discussed and Ross was asked to take back
a message to the effect that the Independent Company
was controlled from Australia and, as they had not been
ordered to surrender, they would not do so. In any case
they preferred to fight rather than be shot unarmed, as
some of the troops had been on the first day of the
landing. Ross set off back to Liquissa and Dili on 17th
March and the Australians began to concoct schemes for
harassing the Japanese.

The River Glano runs from the east near Ailieu to join
the larger River Lois some miles before it runs into the sea
on the north coast and along both sides of the river
Callinan and Turton and their men fought a series of sharp

little actions against much larger Japanese forces, the upshot of which was that forty or more Japanese were killed without loss to the Australians. These actions much impressed the Timorese, who thought the Australians were supermen, and there was no lack of assistance. For a little while the war settled down with the enemy occupying Ermera and probing cautiously southwards while the Australians watched and waited for an opportunity to strike.

They much preferred to kill five or ten Japanese in small actions and suffer no casualties in doing so, since a wounded man would be a serious burden to them. The Japanese solved such problems by shooting their wounded. On one occasion Captain Callinan and Lieutenant Turton and their men set up an ambush on the road near Taco Lulic. They had a group of Timorese with them who were deployed along the road to give advance warning of the Japanese. Then the Australians got into their ambush positions and waited until well into the afternoon with no results. So, since everything appeared to be quiet, the troops moved down from their positions to eat a meal consisting mainly of peanuts and hard-boiled eggs, but in the middle of it their Timorese scouts came running. The Japanese were coming. The troops jumped for their weapons and into their ambush positions while bullets whistled about them, but by the time they were ready to counter-attack the Japanese had retreated down the road to Taco Lulic and so spoilt any chance of an ambush. But this taught them a lesson and the Australians learnt never to rely completely on the Timorese as scouts and never to take all their men out of ambush positions at the same time.

Two days later Japanese could be seen moving about on the Hatu Lia and Ermera roads and a group clustered round a bridge over the Glano River. This promised an ideal target and arrangements for an ambush were made but matters got slightly out of hand when, early in the morning, Corporal Thompson and another sapper were bringing up reserves of explosive and ammunition on ponies on what appeared to be a clear road and, rounding a bend, they saw a Japanese thirty yards away. Both sides dived for cover and then the Japanese turned and ran back down the road. Thompson set up his Bren gun and he spotted several Japanese in a washaway. He opened fire and killed some of them. The others ran on down the road and into another washaway but they were still visible and again Thompson was on target and killed more. Then a truck came into sight and started to turn on the narrow road. As it did so Thompson opened up on the driver and the truck went off the road over the embankment. The Japanese had now recovered their wits and began returning fire with machine-guns and mortars. So Thompson and the other sapper took to the hills and, although the ground made cover difficult, he managed to get near the top of a hill. There a party of Japanese sent to cut him off almost ran into him but the Australians went to ground and, not for the first time, escaped owing to the incredible incompetence of Japanese patrols in this type of country.

So the 'Battles of the Glano' continued, much aided by the local Timorese who would arrange for themselves grandstand views of the ambushes without giving them away to the Japanese. On one occasion Corporal Taylor and four men set up an ambush position above a road which ran below three spurs of the mountain and there ambushed a convoy of trucks. The first truck was wiped out by Bren and submachine-gun fire; the second truck was then engaged and suffered heavy casualties, but the third truck had disgorged Japanese who knew what to do and very soon their machine-gun opened up on Taylor and his men, while other Japanese attacked straight up the hill

towards the small ambushing party. The Australians withdrew hurriedly under fire, but the man carrying the Bren
gun was in great difficulty climbing the steep hillside
when, suddenly, two Timorese appeared, whipped the
Bren off his shoulder and tore off up the hill. When the
party had reached a place of safety the Timorese appeared
with the gun. It was support such as this which gave the
Japanese little chance of success.

The Japanese now decided that the Australians, whom
they estimated to be of the order of 300, although in fact
there were only twenty-three of them, must be wiped out
and on 24 April Captain Callinan got word that they were
going to attack his advanced headquarters on a bare ridge
at Lete Foho which was itself overlooked by the high
country to the north. So the force moved out of Lete
Foho, one half going towards Atsabe and the other to
Ainaro. Callinan, who liked to see things for himself,
stayed behind, doing a kind of hide-and-seek through
Lete Foho, and was very nearly captured, but eventually
removed himself to Lieutenant Turton's patrol at Atsabe.

It was at this stage that Captain Callinan received a
signal from Major Spence which proved a tremendous
morale-builder – contact had at last been established with
Australia. This had been done by the creation from two
low-powered Army transmitter sets and other odds and
ends of a transmitter powerful enough to drown the
transmitters operating in northern Australia. The set,
which was christened 'Winnie the War Winner', was the
creation of Captain Parker and Signaller Loveless, who
was responsible for the technical side, although suffering
badly from malaria. It took two months to make and the
strain was tremendous as parts had to be improvised,
stolen and made, so much so that Loveless became very ill
and had to be evacuated, but his name should not be
forgotten as the creation of the set resulted in help flowing

in from Australia, when all hope for the Independent Company was a Hudson which flew low over Bobonaro and was greeted with much delight by the Timorese who shouted,

'It's one of ours!'

There followed a drop at Mape where Brigadier Veale had his headquarters, and from then on the link with Australia was channelled through headquarters, while the Independent Company did the fighting. The first sea link was through a small ship named the *Kuru*. She was commanded by Lieutenant Bennett, RANVR, and was a modest 55 tons. She was fitted with a device which enabled her to hold the smoke she emitted and then release it at will, so as to avoid the telltale stream of smoke which might be spotted by the enemy. This little ship shuttled back and forth from the Services Reconnaissance Base at Darwin thirteen times in all, carrying supplies and personnel and later taking off troops and civilians from Timor. Lieutenant Bennett was one of the unsung heroes of the Timor operation. A quiet man with a modest and charming personality, his services were of inestimable value but performed so unobtrusively that they were taken for granted. Without him and his twenty-man crew aboard the *Kuru* the Independent Company would have been very hard put to it.

One of her visits brought Captains Broadhurst and Wylie, both in Force 136. They had been in the Malayan Police Force and, together with others who had knowledge of Malaya, were being trained to return there under cover to organize resistance, carry out raids and provide information. They established themselves at the east end of the island with the assistance of the very capable Portuguese administrator, Senhor Pires, and set about creating the force which did so much to help the final recovery of Malaya from the Japanese. They had a direct wireless link with Darwin and acted without reference to the Independent Company.

By the end of April, 1942, the reorganization of the Australian Forces was complete and a line about 60 miles long was manned by some 300 fighting troops. From this small force harassment of the enemy continued. Lieutenant Rose, for example, receiving continual reports from the Timorese that a Japanese outpost of twenty men had established themselves in a village in the high country, decided to investigate and, if true, to wipe out the Japanese. To that end he and a soldier from his section 'blacked up' with soot and dirt from the local cooking pots and set off with two guides for the village which consisted of five huts. A cautious reconnaissance by the guides proved that the Japanese occupied two. They had set no sentry and were probably asleep when Rose and his 'tommy gunner' treated both huts to a shower of grenades and bursts of fire. There was no reply. By dawn Rose and his gunner were back in hiding, watching for any movement, but none came and later reports from the villagers confirmed the wiping out of the whole Japanese party, which was not replaced.

There were often two or three successful raids each week, which resulted in small casualties for the Japanese on each raid, but when these casualties were totted up they provided a remarkable total, and the effect on Japanese morale was enormous. The Japanese told the Timorese that the Australians were devils who jumped out of the ground, killed some Japanese and then disappeared. The Australians were blamed for everything, including the cutting of the throats of eleven Japanese soldiers by Japanese marines in Dili after an argument.

Another noteworthy thrust which the Japanese ascribed to the Australians was brought about by two Portuguese 'deportados'. These men were part of a group exiled by the Portuguese government to Timor who had been living in a hut near the waterfront in Dili. They had noticed that when it rained the Japanese anti-aircraft gun crews took shelter in a nearby hut, so, one night, having fortified themselves with much rice wine and with the rain teeming down, out they went, removed the guns from their mountings and threw them into the sea. The subsequent uproar was amazing. Dili was turned upside down in the search for the marauding Australians and next day three Japanese soldiers were shot as an example to the others not to leave their posts.

Perhaps the raid that caused the greatest alarm to the Japanese was that carried out by Lieutenants Laidlaw and Garnet on Dili. Laidlaw's platoon was well established at Remexio, south-east of and overlooking Dili, and his raid had several objectives. First and foremost it was to draw the enemy's attentions away from the west and south coast areas. Then to try and rescue Private Ryan who had been captured near the aerodrome in the early days of the fighting, and lastly to create as much havoc as possible with the twenty men available. The party 'blacked up' with soot and grime and late in the afternoon of 15 May they moved down to Dili. The usual sentries were unexpectedly absent and after dark the raiders moved through the wire and into Dili. Garnet's party took up positions near the beach to act as a cover and to create the maximum fire diversion as soon as Laidlaw and his section started their action. There were deep drains on either side of the main street and the Australians made use of these for cover until Laidlaw, who was reconnoitring a Japanese machine-gun post, was forced to shoot a Japanese who appeared suddenly. Chaos and confusion followed as the raiders shot up the buildings and the Japanese; the covering party on the beach poured in a withering fire making the Japanese think a large-scale attack had been launched from the beach. A general alarm was sounded, reinforcements were rushed to the beach and firing in all directions continued for some hours after the Australians had withdrawn.

Thereafter Dili was put in a state of siege and soon Remexio was subjected to a full-scale attack by some 400 Japanese troops supported by artillery. The town was successfully occupied, but as there were no Australians there the victory was somewhat hollow. On the night after the Japanese had withdrawn the Australians were back again and the usual observation posts were manned. The Independent Company was achieving the aims of its training.

The Japanese had now occupied the whole of Dutch Timor and early in May they moved out from Dili to Ailieu, causing the Australians considerable concern, for a drive from Ailieu to the south coast would have prevented the Australians moving eastwards and would threaten the whole of the carefully built-up organization. Fortunately the move was only a sortie and after two days they withdrew once more to Dili, giving the Australians time to do all possible damage to the road south from Ailieu to hinder any attempt by the enemy to advance southwards.

The deportados continued to help the Australians and in one particularly daring raid they moved a valuable transceiver from under the noses of the Japanese and so provided a useful standby to the hard-pressed 'Winnie'. It was then, also, that the deportados formed a group actively to help the fighting troops, christened 'The International Brigade'. They fought throughout the campaign and were of great assistance.

The RAAF had been assiduous in dropping supplies and now switched, on demand, to bombing Japanese concentrations. They also escorted the Catalina flying boats which were extremely useful in ferrying people in and out of Timor from the south coast; in so doing they shot down five Zero fighters. One of their missions was to extract Brigadier Veale, the senior Dutch Officer Colonel van Straten and three badly wounded men.

The departure of the Brigadier meant a reorganization of command. Major Spence was promoted to Lieutenant-Colonel and took over command of the Force, while Captain Callinan was promoted to Major and took over command of the augmented Independent Company with Captain Baldwin as second-in-command. Captain Braemour was appointed to command the Dutch troops operating in the south-west corner of Portuguese Timor and patrolling into south-eastern Dutch Timor.

News reached the Australians that the Japanese had brought into Dili some specially trained guerrilla troops from Malaya who were to hunt down the Australians and the Dutch and were led by an individual known as the 'Singapore Tiger'. Not long after a Japanese patrol, one hundred strong, set out from Dili towards Remexio and ran into an ambush set by Corporal Aitkin. The Japanese betrayed considerable nervousness, but not so the leading man who swaggered along as though he owned the area. Naturally enough, when the ambush party opened fire, he was the first casualty and the rest of the Japanese fled without firing a shot. Reports from Dili told of great consternation among the Japanese and amusement in the town among the Portuguese and Timorese because the great 'Tiger' had been out once and had been shot. Nothing more was heard or seen of the Japanese special troops.

At this time Ainaro, the mission centre of the Portuguese colony, housed the Independent Company hospital, a convalescent centre, a reinforcement training depot and the local Portuguese administration. It was from there that Major Callinan and Major Chisholm set out to tour

all their platoons, co-ordinating their arrangements and
fixing rallying points in the event of dispersal for any
reason. It was this continued ability to disperse and
regroup which frustrated the Japanese efforts to wipe out
the force.

On their return they found Mr Ross waiting for them.
He told Major Callinan that he had been summoned by
the new Japanese Consul, a man of some culture, who
told him that the Japanese Commander wished him to
convey once again to the Australians an offer of surrender. He had heard that they were in distress and had
himself seen through his binoculars an Australian on a hill
who was not wearing a shirt; it was clear that the
Australians must be in an unfortunate state! Ross thought
it right to tell the Consul that he did not think the
Australians would surrender because they knew that the
few who had been captured in February had been killed
by the Japanese. The next day he had been summoned to
appear before the Commander of the Japanese forces, a
full colonel, who was most indignant at the reflection cast
on the behaviour of Japanese soldiers towards their
prisoners. He said that neither he, nor any of the soldiers
under his command, had ever killed prisoners, and that he
personally had accepted the surrender of Lieutenant-
Colonel Scott at Ambon.

As a token of his sincerity the Commander had prepared a statement, signed both by himself and by the
Japanese Consul, guaranteeing treatment of prisoners in
accordance with International Law and this had been
handed to Ross to give to the officer commanding the
Australian Forces. He also sent his compliments to the
Australian Commander and asked Ross to convey his
admiration for the fight which the Australians had been
keeping up. He said, however, that if they were real
soldiers they would come into Dili and fight it out like

men. Ross had told him that that was unlikely and the Japanese Commander had replied that in that case he would go into the hills and get them. Ross said that there were not sufficient Japanese soldiers in Dili and the Commander surprised him by agreeing and said that from his own experience in Manchuria it required ten regular soldiers to kill each guerrilla but he had added that he would get what was required. Next day Ross, with Major Callinan, moved to Force Headquarters at Mape where his message and other information was passed on to Australia. Nothing more was heard of the demand for surrender and, since Ross was in very bad physical condition and had not promised to return to Dili, he and the Dutch Consul and his wife who had escaped from Dili were evacuated on the *Kuru*, fortified, as was Major Callinan, by the rice whisky brewed by Senhor Lopez, who owned the plantation at Cunasa through which they had to pass to reach Beco.

There followed a relatively quiet period, but it was vital for the Australians to maintain the initiative and Darwin was asked to send 3-inch mortars to enable Dili to be subjected to sudden bombings which might lure the Japanese out to fight in the hills. It says a great deal for the effectiveness of the Australian campaign when it is realized that now they had to try and annoy the enemy sufficiently to get him to fight, in sharp contrast to previous months.

In July it became clear that the Japanese were going over to the attack. They were buying up large numbers of horses and calling in numbers of Timorese; added to which, some Timorese were turning hostile and attacking carriers loyal to the Australians. It was on 9 August that the storm broke. It was a fine Sunday morning and people were gathering in Bobonaro for market when Japanese planes, with their characteristic surging sound, came over

and began a leisurely and methodical bombing of Bobonaro, Mape and Beco. The Timorese scattered in all
directions and the Australians prepared for action on all
fronts. The next day a convoy consisting of two small
transports escorted by a large destroyer appeared off the
coast at Beco and a little later the bombing of other towns
throughout Portuguese Timor began, obviously with the
intention of lowering local morale among the Portuguese
and the Timorese. Force headquarters at Mape dispersed
and moved to Bobonaro as it was the easiest way of
getting to the east end of the island.

The Japanese plan began to unfold: there were four
main columns made up of some 2,500 troops driving in at
known Australian posts. Two columns moved out of Dili
and one began pushing Laidlaw and his men back from
Remexio and Liltai to the south, while the other pushed
through Lau Lora, Ailieu and Maubisse. Another drive
came from Manatuto to the north, and from Dutch Timor
came two other columns, one through the Dutch positions
at Fatu Lulic, Fatu Mean and Tilomar, and the other
through Memo and Maliana towards Bobonaro. There
were also landings at Beco but those were largely nullified
by an RAAF attack which set fire to one ship and caused
the others to disperse. Plans for such a situation had been
made some time before and were now put into practice.
The important thing was not to get boxed in.

The Timorese were becoming more and more treacherous, giving away ambush positions to the Japanese and
refusing food, and in some cases actively assisting the
enemy by attacking the Australians. The platoons leap-
frogged their way towards Ainaro, keeping radio contact
all the way and being given away by the Timorese, who
had clearly decided that the Japanese were going to win.
The headquarters unit spent the night of 14 August on the
crest of a range no more than fifteen feet wide. To add to

their misfortune it was very cold, there was a thick mist and at dusk a severe earth tremor. All that there was to eat and drink for a group of nine Australians and eleven Timorese was two emergency rations, a small tin of bully beef and two pints of water. The next night the group crept stealthily into Ainaro, expecting to meet the Japanese. Instead they found a half-caste Chinese preparing food and at last were able to make a respectable meal. Later the man was found to have been spying for the Japanese and as it was his second offence he was shot.

Things got progressively worse and it was clear that to escape the closing net the Force would have to move rapidly eastwards. Finally, on 19 August, the hospital at Same was moved and standing patrols put across all tracks, but next day all platoons reported no enemy in the area. This astonishing piece of news meant that the patrols had to chase back westwards to keep contact with the retreating enemy to know his precise location. Why the enemy chose to retreat at this juncture has never been clear. They may have run out of rations; certainly the Australians remained as elusive as ever, while enemy casualties had been severe. Meanwhile, the platoons which had kept a whole regiment under pressure for ten days still could not relax. Food had to be procured, batteries charged, ammunition replenished and reconnaissance continued. The Hudsons of the RAAF worked magnificently during this crucial period, flying in supplies, bombing and strafing round the clock. From then on all patrols had to be fighting patrols, always expecting attack from the local people, who, if not actively hostile, despite excellent work by the Portuguese administration, were scared to help.

Before the Japanese started their August drive they had spread anti-white propaganda, which included the Portuguese. It did not take much of this propaganda, backed by bribery and physical compulsion for non-compliance with Japanese orders, to release the underlying savagery in the Timorese. One of the results of this was that the Chéfé de Posto of Maubisse, who had taken refuge with the local Timorese chief during the bombing of Maubisse, was betrayed and murdered. Before being killed he was tortured and had his hands and feet cut off, dying in agony. This event greatly shocked the local people since the Chéfé had been a good man who looked after his area well and had obviously been killed because he was a white man.

The Portuguese administration was not one to allow its own people to behave in this manner and they called up their army of some 200 Timorese troops with Portuguese officers and NCOs, divided into two companies and armed with rifles and Vickers machine-guns. At the same time the people in the surrounding areas were ordered to arm and prepare for war. This was much approved of as they enjoyed a fight and because the people round Maubisse were pagans while those round Same and Ainaro were Christians, the idea of 'policing' the Maubisse area suited them very well. At a given signal there was a concentrated drive into the Maubisse area from the south and east and the Australians soon saw that, compared with what was now happening, the Japanese efforts at subduing an area were child's play. The villages were burnt; the crops were destroyed; the women, children and animals became spoils of the victors; everywhere lay bloated corpses and a foul smell drifted over all. The Australians did not want to become involved in this local war and strict orders were given to all the troops to remain neutral, but to let it be known that any unfriendly acts by the local population would be punished in such a way that Portuguese punishment would look tame by comparison.

The Japanese woke up to the fact that, unless they took

some action, the Portuguese would once more have control over their own part of Timor and that this would be to the advantage of the Australians. Pressure was brought to bear on the Portuguese government, via the Portuguese governor in Dili, where he was virtually a prisoner, not allowed to receive reports from his officials but permitted only to send out orders which suited the Japanese. As a result the Portuguese army was withdrawn, while the Japanese occupied Bobonaro; from that moment the Portuguese administration began to fade out, leaving the Australians to assume more responsibility over the local people.

On 16 September, 1942, HMAS *Vigilant* appeared with a small advance party from the 2/4th Independent Company which was to reinforce the 2/2nd. It was made up of Major Walker, the Company Commander, and three commanders plus one other officer from each of the three platoons. The officers went to their equivalent platoons in the 2/2nd, while Major Walker went to see Colonel Spence and later to confer with Major Callinan. Captain Baldwin was in charge of the arrangements for the reception of the rest of the 2/4th Company and this involved the collection of over 400 horses and Timorese and keeping them under cover and fed until they were required. To add to their troubles the ship bringing the 2/4th was a day late.

Quite suddenly an immense bow wave swept into view and HMAS *Voyager*, a destroyer with a great record at Tobruk in the Middle East campaign, came in very close to the rapidly shelving shore. As the tide ebbed, the destroyer bumped and in no time at all was firmly aground. The disembarkation continued but it proved impossible to get the *Voyager* off and all troops stood by for the discovery of the landing by the morning Japanese reconnaissance plane. Sure enough it came, it saw and returned at high speed to Dili. Soon after, Japanese bombers came over, dropped one hundred bombs, scored one hit and received a very hostile reception from the anti-aircraft fire on *Voyager*, which shot down one plane. The commanding officer ordered *Voyager* to be blown up and this was done after the heavy Vickers machine-guns and other suitable armament and stores had been given to the Independent Companies.

The Japanese aircraft also strafed the beachhead but, owing to the efficiency with which Baldwin and his party worked, not one Timorese was hit nor were any stores lost. In fact the Timorese accepted the stranding of the *Voyager* as part of the operation. It had done its job; the Australians did not want it any more; therefore they had left it on the beach.

As soon as Darwin heard of the stranding of the *Voyager* two corvettes were dispatched to pick up the crew and, although comparatively slow, they completed their task, at the same time taking with them the sick and wounded.

As was to be expected, the Japanese mounted attacks in strength which were able to push through to the south coast and examine *Voyager*, losing heavily from ambushes as they did so. They then returned to their bases, allowing the somewhat disorganized Independent Companies to regroup.

The Japanese now began an intensive propaganda campaign among the Timorese and it became more and more difficult to obtain food. They also told the Timorese that all white men, and this included the Portuguese, must be killed and they initiated a new tactic whereby their patrols were led by fifty or sixty Timorese who would, inevitably, become the first casualties in any ambush.

To make themselves less dependent on the Timorese the Australians began to purchase horses for all platoons to make them more mobile, and in the process discovered that the Timorese were expert horse thieves and good at selling the same horse twice, a practice which ceased abruptly when a thrice-convicted seller was shot. The Japanese had by now realized that the Portuguese, whether in administrative posts or not, would create centres of resistance and they therefore put forward the idea of a 'neutral zone' – an idea peculiarly their own since any Portuguese outside the Maubara-Liquissa area to the west of Dili, after 15 November, 1942, would be treated as though actively assisting the Australians. The Portuguese distrusted the idea instinctively and asked whether the Australians could evacuate their women and children, difficult though this might be.

Colonel Callinan (who had been promoted to command of Sparrow Force when Colonel Spence left for Australia; the name Sparrow Force had been changed to Lancer Force for security reasons) then went to discuss the matter with a representative gathering of Portuguese and was told that, if the women and children could be sent to Australia, the men would stay and fight. He contacted Darwin on the matter and, pending a reply, arranged for the Portuguese women and children to be moved to a place of safety to the east. When he got back to his headquarters, he was not amused to find a message from Australia stating that, pending a policy decision in Australia, all offers to evacuate the Portuguese or disarm them must be suspended. Callinan replied in terms which made it clear that he did not appreciate obstacles placed in the way of conducting the war in Timor from a distance of some thousand miles. Nothing further was heard on the subject.

It was becoming more and more obvious that the strain of fighting was beginning to exhaust the 2/2nd Company, despite the magnificent way the 2/4th were taking up the burden, but they too were suffering from lack of food and what there was was of a very poor quality. The 2/2nd had been fighting continuously for over nine months and all but twenty men had had malaria, many had had dysentery and pleurisy at the same time. Yet they had never given up and had given an incredibly good account of themselves. Three hundred men had continuously engaged and beaten off an overwhelming number of Japanese and turned a forlorn effort into an outstandingly successful campaign which, at that date, had resulted in the killing of over 1,000 Japanese for the loss of twenty-six Australians. In all the many remarkable episodes of the war there are few which match the performance of the 2/2nd Company in terms of sheer courage and military skill. Yet this was not to be the end of their great saga.

The Japanese now had an overwhelming numerical superiority and could afford to take their time. Slowly and methodically they established themselves along the northeast coast, developing Baucau as a port so that ships no longer discharged at Dili. At the same time new airstrips and dumps of supplies were established and the Timorese were organized to attack the areas held by the Australians. This they did by destroying the villages and crops of any Timorese who would not obey them.

Now the Australians were restricted in areas in which, before, they had been able to move freely and, despite all kinds of tricks, they were unable to draw the Japanese into ambushes. A typical case was that of a corporal who 'blacked up' and, clad in a sarong, mingled with a crowd of loyal islanders near a group of Japanese. Then he slipped a tommy gun from under his sarong and created havoc before getting away unscathed. Even so there was no pursuit.

Despite the great assistance from the RAAF, using Beaufighters and Mitchells, and also from the United

States Airforce, the numerical strength of the Japanese, fronted as they were by screens of Timorese, prevented the Australians getting at them and gradually they were forced back towards the east. The platoons of the 2/4th Company, in particular, were hard pressed by the need to be constantly moving to avoid encirclement, but the observation posts on the north coast continued to operate successfully. The Australian post to the east of Dili was under continual harassment by enemy patrols and bombing, and found it very difficult to produce any real results, but to the west O'Connor and his platoon continued to carry out ambushes on the north coast road which caused the Japanese much disruption and concern.

Colonel Spence and other officers who had returned from Timor to Australia had made it clear that the 2/2nd Company and their Dutch allies were so exhausted that their effectiveness as a fighting machine was rapidly deteriorating and in early November an order was sent to Colonel Callinan to make ready for the withdrawal of the Dutch and the 2/2nd Company and to state what staff he wanted to keep at headquarters. This put Colonel Callinan in an agonizing dilemma; there were thirty or forty 'originals' at Headquarters and he could not ask them to remain while the rest of the 2/2nd Company was evacuated. In the end he solved the problem by deciding that he and Captain Baldwin would remain and the gaps in the headquarters staff would be filled from the 2/4th Company.

There was, suddenly, an immense and complicated move to arrange: the whole of the 2/2nd had to be withdrawn and replaced by the 2/4th. The Dutch troops, the Portuguese from Alas and some nuns and priests had to be moved down to the Qualan River and all this without the Japanese getting an inkling of what was happening. In the first phase the Company was to move to

the beach at Betano and there protect the evacuation of
the Dutch troops and the others.

At 2200 on the night of the evacuation recognition
signals were exchanged with a ship at sea which turned out
to be the 55-ton *Kuru* but without the corvettes *Castlemaine* and *Armidale* which were to have brought over a
new detachment of Dutch troops together with some
Australians. The *Kuru* had a crew of twenty and, after
unloading stores, it took some seventy passengers, chiefly
women and children, and then departed. Later signals
explained that the corvettes had been engaged by
Japanese aircraft and had been delayed arriving off
Betano. There they had received no recognition signals
and so had departed. Next morning the *Kuru* was attacked
by bombers and fighters but managed to survive and
contacted the corvettes. The refugees were transferred to
the *Castlemaine* which returned to Darwin while the
Armidale and the *Kuru* made another attempt to land the
Dutch and Australians, but Japanese aircraft continued to
attack the two ships and, tragically, the *Armidale* was
sunk, taking with her the Dutch and Australians.

At the time Colonel Callinan knew nothing of this, but
eventually a signal told him of the loss of the troops and
that the pick-up of the 2/2nd Company would be delayed
by twenty-four hours. This led to Colonel Callinan asking
for a further day's delay as he reorganized his sparse
forces to cover the gaps which would have been filled by
the Dutch. Things were not made easier by an unexpected
Japanese attack at Same which resulted in a loss of rifles,
pack horses and vital codes. The enemy knew that something was afoot and began to close in, making it necessary
to change the beachhead from Betano to the Qualan
River and this time it was the Dutch destroyer *Djerk
Hedes* which came in on time and, despite bad landing
conditions, the remaining Dutch and Portuguese, together

with Captain Dunkley's medical unit and Lieutenant Doig's platoon, were embarked and the destroyer sailed for Darwin in less than two hours.

There were now some thirty thousand Japanese on Timor and, as Colonel Callinan remarked, 'the air was becoming a little stuffy'. The south coast had been increasingly infested by the Japanese and there was left a strip of about twenty miles from which supplies could be obtained, but in the centre and north of the island it was extremely difficult to obtain food or to control the local population. All patrols for a long time had been fighting patrols and had had to operate with a wary eye on the local people in case of treachery, which greatly reduced their effectiveness not only as fighting units but from the strain on their nerves, the lack of sleep and the need to keep on the move.

On 4 January a message was received asking how long it would take to concentrate the force for evacuation at any given point. The reply 'three clear days' went back the same night. The following night Colonel Callinan was instructed to concentrate the Force for evacuation on the night 9/10 January at a point to be nominated by him. There was no more sleep that night. There would be no rearguards and, unless great care was taken, there would be a running battle down to the point of evacuation. Colonel Callinan and Captain Baldwin were the only two of the 'originals' left and, as it was expected that they would go back to Australia, their moves would be watched closely and discussed widely by the troops.

The move of the platoons was begun slowly and unobtrusively and the hospital under Captain Hennessy was brought to a point near Quicras – the point, equidistant between the Japanese advancing from east and west, from which it was planned to carry out the embarkation, but this roused no concern among the population since there were over one hundred Portuguese refugees there who could profit from the presence of the doctor. More arms and training were given to the local Timorese and a drop of mail was arranged. There seemed to be no leakage of information to the Japanese and they had no inkling of what was happening.

Colonel Callinan now gave some thought to whether any good purpose would be served by leaving a small Australian unit on the island for he was loath to throw away the hard-earned results of the work done by the Force since February, 1942. First there had been the struggle for existence during February, March and April; then a serious threat to the Japanese during May, June and July, followed by a fight for life against a Japanese regiment in August; then the period after the stranding of the *Voyager* when the Force was prepared to withstand an assault, followed by continuous fighting against overwhelming odds during October, November and December. Finally he sent a signal to Australia recommending that a small force should remain to carry on reconnaissance and harassment wherever possible.

During the morning of 9 January a message was received from Australia saying that a party of one Lieutenant and twenty other ranks was to remain but Colonel Callinan was to return. Captain Baldwin asked to remain but was overruled and the final composition of the party of volunteers was Lieutenant H. Flood in command, Sergeant Ellwood, the cipher officer, several signallers and non-commissioned officers and the rest privates. Later three members of the Ainaro patrol who had not been able to fight their way to the beachhead in time joined them.

The final move down to the beach started before dawn on 9 January and was difficult because there was only a single track leading from Cledec through open grassland, very vulnerable to air observation. The weather, which usually provided rain in the afternoon, reversed itself so that, instead of remaining under cover until the morning Japanese air patrol was over, they had to move as fast as possible to avoid being caught in the flooded rivers. Clouds began to come over soon after first light and it was fortunate that they did so because not long after a Japanese Zero appeared out of the cloud at about 1,000 ft. Everyone froze, the plane passed, changed course rapidly and flew over Cledec. The tension and the stillness were immense. Would it turn back? When it continued to the north the collective sigh of relief was plainly audible. After eleven o'clock the rain began to deluge the marching column and went on for an hour, settling eventually into a steady drizzle, but it was warm and to the Timorese and Australians nothing out of the ordinary.

Quicras, a few huts set in a malarial swamp, was not in use permanently but served as a halt for a midday meal. Then came the last leg of the journey through swamps which varied from knee to chest high in depth. The track led through and over slippery mangrove roots, coated in stinking mud, but by five o'clock in the evening the whole force and its stores was spread along the beach, concealed in the scrub which came down to high water mark. Everything was ready and the force settled down to wait, with the criados and the troops who had been their masters making their sad farewells and exchanging gifts.

After dark three large signal fires were prepared and a signalling lamp set up above the beach which was long and straight but shelved steeply. A surf of five to six feet and a strong current setting to the east were going to make embarkation difficult, but there was no better place. At 1130 the fires were lit and on the stroke of midnight the first recognition signal came from the darkness out to sea.

It was answered and repeated. All was set and, after the
minutes had dragged on apparently interminably, the
sound of motor-boats was heard and a line of flat-
bottomed folding plywood boats could just be seen
beyond the surf. The first boat came through and was
swamped; the second boat got through and was loaded
with women and children but capsized getting back, only
to be righted by heroic efforts. Gradually more boats
came in and took off the sick and wounded, then the
troops. But there were still 160 troops left on the beach
when the destroyer signalled that no more boats could be
sent and it looked as though all the previous planning had
been wasted. Colonel Callinan had foreseen such an
eventuality and had arranged for weapons and equipment
to be stacked ready to use if anyone had to remain ashore.

On the destroyer someone must have put the case very
forthrightly for more boats came in and as the tide ebbed
the surf became less boisterous and an efficient launching
party under Lieutenant O'Connor began to get the troops
on to the boats. Further alarms from the destroyer caused
some men to try and swim out beyond the breakers but
that proved useless in the darkness and steep, short seas.
Then more boats came in and Lieutenant Flood and his
men packed them to capacity and shoved them out
beyond the surf. Captain Baldwin went in one and Colonel Callinan in the last boat to leave. From the boats a
cheer went up for the beach party and on the wind came a
faint reply.

As the last soldier was hauled aboard sailors cut loose
the boat and the destroyer, HMAS *Arunta*, newly built
and commissioned in Australia, was on her way, soon
working up to thirty knots straight for Darwin. There was
less than one hour left before dawn. Colonel Callinan
must have presented a far from credible picture when he
reported to Commander Morrow – bearded, wet through,

in a dirty pair of shorts with no boots or stockings, hat or equipment, he was scarcely recognizable as a Force Commander. After a bath he turned in to sleep for sixteen hours.

On the beach the party under Lieutenant Flood, now known as 'S' Force, began to clear up and to try and hide evidence of the embarkation. Then the Force moved off to a camp site on a coffee plantation near Fatu Berli, leaving the criados to fight and argue over the gear left on the beach, arguments often settled by shots. Lieutenant Flood's orders were to observe and report on Japanese activities and to avoid direct contact with the enemy except in self-defence, but time was needed for the group to organize supplies and to establish themselves in an area where the Timorese would support and conceal them. But the Japanese lost no time in scouring the district and a few days later a strong enemy patrol drove through the coffee plantation. A running fight ensued during which most of the wireless equipment was lost and, worst of all, the codes disappeared on a bolting pony. The party regrouped, managed to put together a new set, rather on the lines of 'Winnie the War Winner', and contacted Darwin.

The Japanese were not going to leave them in peace and another attack developed towards Soibada. In getting the radio equipment away the pony carrying the gear was shot, fell into a torrent and was carried away. Again all contact with Darwin was lost and the small force broke up, making their way south-east under constant Japanese pressure. Food was extremely scarce and one group existed for five days on a small quantity of buffalo hide and some sago, while malaria made itself felt in all of them.

Gradually, through the help of the Timorese and refugee Portuguese, the groups coalesced and managed to contact 'Z' Special Force under Captains Broadhurst and Wylie, who had been gathering intelligence and organizing the Timorese at the eastern end of Timor. They had with them Lieutenants Cashman, Grimson and Thomas and Sergeant Smith, and they too were being actively hunted by the Japanese. Their radio would transmit but would not receive and as soon as the two parties found an area in which they could conceal themselves a message was sent to Darwin asking for a new wireless set, batteries and food. The ever-faithful Hudsons came over a few nights later and dropped food and batteries but no new wireless. This was reported to Darwin in vivid language and two days later the Hudsons re-appeared with more food and two sets. Friendly Timorese now brought news of the Japanese converging on the area and the party had to move continuously through the malarial swamps, not daring to light a fire in case it gave them away.

It was clear that neither of the two groups was able to carry out its mission of supplying information and all were in an exhausted condition. A message was sent to Darwin explaining the situation and asking permission to leave the island. This was given and the evacuation was fixed for 10 February near the mouth of the Dilor River which meant a delay of some days during which Japanese patrols began converging on the area. The two groups, under almost unbearable tension, moved into position towards dusk and as the light was fading five Hudsons came over and dropped rubber dinghies, but when these had been recovered it was found that all but one had burst valves. The one usable dinghy was made ready and on the seaward side of the scrub above the narrow beach they hung a white cloth to be sighted by the submarine which was to pick them up.

After dusk a submarine surfaced and recognition signals were exchanged. The dinghy was paddled out through the heavy surf to the submarine which proved to be the USS

Gudgeon, a craft with a very successful and gallant record of attacks on enemy shipping. The situation was explained and the *Gudgeon* inflated one of her own much larger dinghies and soon all the troops were off the beach, after giving their last gifts to their criados who had stood by them so well and had never faltered in their devotion and unselfishness. Eight days later the *Gudgeon* brought the parties into Fremantle. 'S' Force had kept going against incredible odds for a month and a day after the 2/4th Company had been evacuated and with their return the last of the Australians in Lancer Force had left Timor.

Although the Japanese now had no opposition to their rule on Timor, the island was too important strategically for the Allies, and in particular the Australians, not to know what was going on there and it fell to 'Z' Special to take up the task.

In their mission codenamed 'Lizard' Captains Broadhurst and Wylie had already established contacts near Suai and Beasso towards the east end of Timor before leaving the island on 10 February, 1943. They had operated from the Services Reconnaissance Base which occupied the old quarantine station twelve miles west of Darwin and was known as Lugger Maintenance Section. This base had been established by Captain J. Chipper, but he was replaced by Major Bingham who, in addition to his other qualities, spoke Dutch. The base was a large one with a stream of operational units passing through it. There were, for example, Portuguese under Major C. Brandao, who had been brought out of Timor, and a Dutch organization known as NEFIS, operating throughout the Indies. A special area was set aside for Timorese and other indigenous people captured during raids and they were under the care of Lieutenant Holland, AIF, in private life a timber man from New Guinea. There were good marine facilities used by the 'Snake' ships and other craft such as the *Krait*, and a slipway and repair workshops for we also carried out trials on some of the peculiar craft mentioned earlier. The base staff with its planners, liaison officers, quartermasters and others was a mixture of Australians, British and one American.

The base or LMS, as it was called, was a closed area but cordial if remote relations were maintained with the large base at Darwin and others nearby, for there were times when concerted action was necessary.

After the final withdrawal of the Independent Companies from Timor the first party to go back was given the codename 'Lagarto'. It was led by a Captain Santos, Portuguese Forces, with Lieutenant Pirez as his second-in-command; they had with them as signaller Sergeant Ellwood, AIF, who was later commissioned in the field. Soon after landing on the south coast, and contrary to instructions, they gathered a party of wives and friends, including children, and moved slowly across the island to the north coast. Such a large group and the methods by which they operated made the result inevitable. They were all captured by the Japanese and Sergeant Ellwood's last message was in clear. It said:

'Japanese are attacking. Am burying radio.'

They had been captured somewhere to the east of Dili and after the party went off the air two challenge messages were sent. When Ellwood did not come up with a reply, a third message with the challenge word 'Slender' repeated deliberately three times was sent from Services Reconnaissance Department in Melbourne. Meanwhile the Japanese had recovered the radio and, by means of torture, had made Ellwood give them the code and so received all the messages sent by base. When they found a message with a word repeated three times and clearly an authenticator, they tortured Ellwood again until he was forced to reveal what it meant.

Some six weeks after Ellwood's message in clear, to the vast surprise of Darwin, who did not know what had been done by Melbourne, Ellwood once more came up and this time he explained that he had escaped into the mountains and that all was reasonably well. No one in Darwin had any reason to believe otherwise since they were never told by Melbourne what had happened. Either those in charge in Melbourne were idiots in interpreting what had happened or else they deliberately concealed the fact that Lagarto was compromised. If they had had the courage to let Darwin know what had happened Services Reconnaissance Department might well have been put out of business as far as getting agents into Timor went, and so have lost all credibility, *but* a number of valuable lives would have been saved.

It is very difficult to believe that, despite what had happened, Melbourne authorized another party, codenamed 'Cobra', and consisting of Lieutenant Cashman, Sergeant Liversidge and three Portuguese to go in by sea on the south coast. Ellwood was told to go down and meet them on the beach, lighting three fires as a signal. The result was entirely predictable: the whole party was captured; the Portuguese were executed and the Australians were held prisoner. One more party under Lieutenant Grimson was inserted by sea, after two abortive attempts at a river mouth on the south coast towards the east end of the island. As Ellwood had been advised of their coming the 'friendly' Japanese reception party killed them all. The Japanese then began to enjoy themselves because LMS Darwin continued to supply both Lagarto and Cobra parties with stores on the instructions of the Japanese sent through Ellwood.

In Darwin plans were going ahead for the insertion of further operational groups, since neither Major Bingham nor his Intelligence Officer, Flight-Lieutenant A. Brierley, RAAF, had been told of the previous disasters. The next group of agents was divided into several smaller groups all under the codename 'Sun Fish'. Captain A. D. Stevenson, AIF, who had fought in Timor with the 2/4th Company and had been one of the last to be taken off by

HMAS *Arunta*, was in command. His own party was codenamed 'Sun Lag'; there was also 'Sun Cob', destined for East Timor under Captain Wyn, AIF, who had fought there with the 2/4th Company. 'Sun Able' was commanded by Captain Williams, AIF, and was to drop into the Occussi Enclave on the north coast of Timor. He had a difficult task before him as he did not know the area and there were no contacts awaiting him. 'Sun Baker', under Captain Wilkins, AIF, was to go in near Koepang; 'Sun Charlie' was to drop in on Flores; and 'Sun Dog' on the island of Roti.

They were all to be inserted by parachute and the pilot of the Liberator which was to do the dropping wanted to reconnoitre the dropping zones as some of them were rather close to mountains. To do this he took off on the pretence of a leaflet raid and also took Sun Baker, Sun Charlie and Sun Dog parties to look at their areas. While the aircraft was flying along the north coast of Timor it had the misfortune to encounter a Japanese Anti-Aircraft battery on the move along the coast road and this went into action and shot them down, killing everyone on board. This was a ghastly tragedy which, at the time, was said to have occurred when the Liberator hit a mountain in cloud; it set back operations for a month. Then Sun Able was dropped into its area and, after a few days of heavy and continuous fighting, the party were all killed after accounting for a large number of Japanese.

In the meantime Major Bingham was beginning to have serious doubts about the safety of the code being used. He had, through Major Wigan, a member of his staff, a contact with one of the code intercept stations in Australia and it looked very much from one Japanese signal they had broken that Ellwood was compromised. He said as much to Captain Stevenson, who found it hard to believe but was persuaded by Major Bingham to go in two days early at the chosen place for Sun Lag, Laleia.

Captain Stevenson was familiar with the area into which he, his sergeant and Celestino, a Portuguese, were to drop. His intention was to relieve the Lagarto party and get it out to Australia, then select contact points on either the north or south coasts where stores and/or more operators could be put in. If all went well the party was to carry out reconnaissance of enemy posts and suitable targets and to report on enemy land movements and approximate strength, finally to try and create a local Timorese organization for the purpose of intelligence, propaganda and resistance, with the ultimate object of gaining control of the area.

The party was to go in by statichute drop from a Liberator, which would make two runs, dropping the bodies first and their stores by storpedo on the second run. Lagarto was not to be informed of the insertion. Instead the following message was sent:

A recce for Methos II will be made next two days followed by supply drop at last light on D + 2 STOP Same place and signal STOP Ack.

Methos referred to previous messages of intent.

The drop was signalled for 1 July but Sun Lag went in on 29 June, jumping at 5.50 P.M. to the RV near the Laleia River. Captain Stevenson landed in a tree east of the river and Sergeant Dawson, AIF, and Celestino in a river bed. Within thirty minutes they had all assembled. They found their storpedo, unloaded it and cached the stores and food and then moved to the hideout area. They kept on the move, parallel to and east of the river, and reached Laleia River again after dark. They cached the radio near the river and moved to a point a mile upstream of the point at which Lagarto stores were usually dropped. There Dawson and Celestino remained in hiding, while Stevenson moved on and by dawn was in position on the east bank of the Laleia immediately opposite and within 150 yards of the Lagarto signal lamp position.

By that time Ellwood had been advised from Darwin that the reconnaissance flight (on which Sun Lag had actually come in) had ended in engine trouble and that the live drop would not take place but a stores aircraft would be sent to him.

The early part of 1 July was uneventful, except for an occasional Timorese moving along the river bed, but at 4 P.M. Ellwood appeared, escorted by three Japanese soldiers. He was carrying a Lucas Lamp in its box. He appeared in quite good physical condition and was wearing a clean, green shirt and trousers and a web belt. He sat down on the ground, cross-legged, and the Japanese went into hiding. At 5 P.M. Ellwood set up his lamp and watched the north. Then at dusk he repacked his lamp, a whistle sounded three times from the lamp position and the sentries moved in, two of them within thirty yards of Stevenson.

So it was clear that Ellwood was under coercion and that the code had been compromised. The next two days were occupied in trying to contact LMS, but without success, and the party had to keep moving as they had been seen by local people. On 4 July they discovered that both emergency frequency crystals had fractured, so no wonder that their signals were not getting through.

The next day the party moved up towards the hills which Celestino knew fairly well and he was able to contact the chief of a village, who proved friendly and provided food and a hut in some bamboo 400 yards behind his village. Dawson had by this time managed to contact LMS and explained the position. On 7 July they received instructions to move to the extraction point on the coast. In the meantime Sun Cob had dropped in and, because the code had been compromised but Stevenson had not been able to tell LMS by then, was caught. Under interrogation they gave information which led (so Stevenson discovered later) to a search party for Sun Lag, consisting of a company of Japanese troops, 1,000 Timorese including dogs and a mountain battery. The next few days were hectic in the extreme.

At LMS the *Krait* came into the action once again. She left Darwin under Lieutenant H. Williams, RANVR, at 0750 on Friday, 13 July, and set a course to bring her 25 miles off the extraction point at sunset on 15 July, 1945. The journey was uneventful and, as Timor was sighted at 0700 hours on Sunday, 15 July, the speed was reduced to 4 knots but at 1300 the weather deteriorated, the wind increased to Force 5 and the sea was rough with a long, heavy swell. *Krait* closed to within half a mile of the shore but conditions were too bad for the launching of the rubber boat and consequently she stood out to sea. On Monday, the 16th *Krait* closed the land once again and cruised to and past the extraction point but visibility was very bad and no signal was seen, so once more she stood out to sea. On the 17th there was a little improvement in the weather but again, at the crucial moment, visibility shut down to 30 yards and no signal was seen.

On the 18th there was a considerable improvement in the weather and at 2030 hours the extraction point was reached and, with the *Krait* half a mile offshore, the engine was stopped. The extraction party consisted of a major and a Naval lieutenant, both from British Forces and but lately arrived from SOE in Europe, aided by an Australian sergeant. Visibility was excellent and there was a slight offshore wind with the tide setting to the east. At 2210 hours the engine was put at dead slow ahead and *Krait* cruised slowly to the westward, keeping the land close on the starboard hand for about 3 miles. At 2350 hours she turned on a reciprocal course but the weather had turned foul and visibility was poor but at 0150 hours on Thursday, 19 July a signal apparently made by a torch flashing the letter 'R' was seen bearing to port 90 degrees. The engine was stopped and the rubber dinghy put overboard. There was a delay while the major and lieutenant prepared themselves and a further delay when the major missed the dinghy and fell into the water. While all this was going on regular signals from the shore were seen and answered by a long flash (using a blue shade) and apparently this was acknowledged by a 'T' flash. At 0240 the rubber boat left the *Krait* and at 0320 it returned. The party had lost direction and had not been able to locate the shore signals. It nearly got blown out of the water by failing to answer recognition signals from the *Krait*. In an effort to get the shore party to recommence signalling a further flash was sent from the ship at 0325 but there was no reply. The rubber boat was brought aboard and the *Krait* sailed for Darwin, arriving there at 2210 hours on Saturday, 21 July. The extraction had been a failure. It transpired that Sun Lag had seen the light and gone down to the beach, but, owing to the inept handling of the rubber boat, they were once more in grave danger.

For Sun Lag there followed a harrowing few days. They had calculated their rations to cut out on the first night as they were confident of being picked up, so they were now very short of food, and from the increase in the number of sentry posts and people moving about they knew they were being hunted. They kept moving and Celestino managed occasionally to get food from friends and relatives. Often they were barefoot to avoid leaving bootmarks and between July 24 and 28 they spent their time trying to patch up the masses of blisters, cuts and infections on their feet while Celestino scouted and brought in news and occasionally a little food. He was gravely worried because the Japanese had threatened to kill all his family unless he gave himself up. The radio, which they had hidden before going down to the beach, was taken from its hiding place and contact established with LMS. It was arranged to extract Sun Lag by means of one of the Royal Australian Navy's motor launches and to enable the party to get off to her a Mitchell bomber was to drop a rubber dinghy at dawn on 5 August.

The health of the party had deteriorated and they were very debilitated, so that movement and concealment during the next few days was near agony. The Japanese, it transpired later, had direction-finding equipment monitoring their radio signals, but fortunately the party was dead in between their direction-finding sets and they had the latitude but not the longitude, otherwise it is doubtful whether they could have escaped.

On 4 August the party crossed the road parallel to the beach near the extraction point and were challenged, but in the dim light of early morning they took the bold course and walked straight up the road, round a corner and into the bush, which hid them well. There was no sign of a chase so they contacted LMS and then hid the radio. Sergeant Dawson then succumbed with what seemed to be malaria and became incapable of movement. The other two carried out a reconnaissance and found a suitable point for extraction recognition 400 yards to the west, and eventually the whole party moved there and slept until 0300 hours on 5 August.

The Mitchell bomber came in at 0510 and dropped storpedoes. The one containing food did not open its parachute and was lost, but the one containing the rubber dinghy was found and opened, only to find that the inflating gear was useless. The party then went to the pick-up position on the beach – and within ten minutes a section of Timorese coastguards arrived on the scene. They were unarmed and the party captured them, sat them down, filled them with propaganda and the remains of the chocolate and chose one to go with them as a prisoner. Meanwhile the boat was sighted – HDML *1324*, escorted by two corvettes, HMAS *Parkes* and *Gympie*; this time things were to be done in style.

The extraction was codenamed 'Operation Bream' and was headed by Lieutenant Crombie of Z Special, with five men also of Z Special. The HDML was commanded by Lieutenant R. Evans, RANVR, and made landfall about two miles west of the extraction point before first light, then cruised slowly until at first light they were able to recognize land features such as Tata Mau Mountain. By 0545 they had identified the Dilor River and at 0600 the party on shore had identified them and lit flares which were sighted immediately.

Crombie and his men took in a seven-man and a two-man rubber boat and as the weather was fine they got the Sun Lag party off the beach without difficulty and were on board the HDML and away by 0645. It was just as well, for it transpired that the Japanese had spent the night in villages near the shore and arrived hot-foot on the scene at 9 A.M.

Although Operation Sun Lag had not achieved its objectives, it had proved that the codes being used were compromised, that Ellwood and some others were alive and, from information received, it was able to pass on to the Army in Darwin that the Japanese were moving towards Koepang in some numbers to be taken off Timor, a fact of which the RAAF made good use later.

About the time that various operations were moving out of LMS, Darwin, the Services Reconnaissance Base on Morotai, in the Halmaheras to the north, put in hand Operation Opossum. This operation was mounted at the request of the Dutch Government in exile, which was greatly embarrassed by the fact that the Sultan of Ternate,

the ruler of the Northern Halmaheras, which included
Morotai, had been captured by the Japanese when they
overran his island in 1943 and was being held hostage in
his own castle. The Dutch Government had asked the
Australian High Command if it was possible to rescue him
and they in turn had given the task to Services Reconnaissance Department.

Lieutenant H. E. Josselyn, DSC RNVR, the SRD
Naval Liaison Officer in Morotai, arranged for a patrol
boat of the United States Navy to carry a raiding party
from SRD and, on 8 April, 1945, the party, led by
Lieutenant G. Bosworth, AIF, with eight Australians and
three Dutch officers, landed on the island where the castle
was and, achieving initial surprise, they stormed the
castle, whisking away the Sultan and his family of fifteen.
In the running action that followed Lieutenant Bosworth
was killed, also Private Higginbottom. Eleven of the
enemy were killed, a resistance movement was started and
detailed information was obtained of the enemy strength,
defences and communications on the island of Ternate
and the west-coast lines of the Halmaheras. The Dutch
Government were greatly impressed and grateful.

Planning for new operations at LMS and elsewhere was
going forward and, as the action moved north, the Snake
ships were sent forward to Morotai. The *Krait*, after
having various defects attended to, was preparing to leave
for Morotai when the atom bombs were dropped on Japan
and on 14 August Japan surrendered. At first there was a
stunned disbelief, then, slowly, an enormous reaction as
everywhere people began to readjust to the simple fact
that the war had ended.

In the Philippines, in Malaya, in Dutch New Guinea
and throughout the islands of the Netherlands East
Indies resistance groups had been born and had fought
heroically. In the Philippines they had had the very con-

siderable backing of powerful United States forces but in Malaya their main support had come from the Communist Chinese and in those two territories the guerrillas had proved very decisive factors in the final overthrow of the Japanese. But in Dutch New Guinea and in the East Indies there had never been enough resources to do more than provide a constant source of discomfort to the enemy. Nevertheless the Japanese in all these areas suffered a constant drain on their assets and, owing to the activities of the resistance, their efficiency in dealing with major Allied onslaughts was always being whittled away by the necessity to divert some of their forces to deal with the saboteurs, the guerrilla raids and the general resistance built up against them.

It would be impossible, in the confines of this story, to record with any kind of justice the heroic work of all members of the resistance in South-East Asia, so perhaps a record of what one Special Force managed to achieve may stand as a tribute to them all.

By the end of the war against Japan, Services Reconnaissance Department and its offshoots had grown to a force of 1,500 officers and other ranks, mainly Australians but including many British, New Zealanders, Canadians and South Africans. They had raised and equipped over 6,000 guerrillas in the areas in which operations took place. They had inflicted 1,700 known casualties on the Japanese at a cost of approximately 112 lives.

Eighty-one operations had been carried out behind the enemy lines in every area from Borneo and the China and Malayan coasts to the interiors of Malaya, New Guinea and Timor. Resistance groups had been trained for the Philippines and the Netherlands East Indies and the interiors of Borneo and Sarawak had been reoccupied and won back from the Japanese. It became quite apparent that the Japanese had no answer to these activities.

The extent of the successes achieved during such a short period of secret and unorthodox warfare is in itself a tribute to the courage, determination, endurance and skills displayed by those who took part and it is fitting that the Services Reconnaissance Department memorial at Careening Bay, Garden Island, West Australia, should be also the proud epitaph of those who died in creating and maintaining the Ring of Fire.

Appendix 1

Operation Jaywick

Major Ivan Lyon MBE DSO, the Gordon Highlanders
Lieutenant D. M. N. Davidson DSO RNVR
Lieutenant R. C. Page DSO AIF
Lieutenant H. E. Carse RANVR mentioned in dispatches
Leading Stoker J. P. McDowell DSM RN
Leading Telegraphist H. S. Young RAN mentioned in dispatches
Acting Leading Seaman K. P. Cain RAN mentioned in dispatches
Acting Able Seaman W. G. Falls DSM RAN
Acting Able Seaman A. N. W. Jones DSM RAN
Acting Able Seaman A. W. Huston DSM RAN
Acting Able Seaman F. W. Marsh RAN mentioned in dispatches
Acting Able Seaman M. M. Berryman RAN mentioned in dispatches
Corporal R. G. Morris BEM MM RAMC
Corporal A. Crilley MM AIF

Operation Rimau

Lieutenant-Colonel Ivan Lyon MBE DSO, the Gordon Highlanders
Lieutenant Commander D. M. N. Davidson DSO RNVR
Captain R. C. Page DSO AIF
Lieutenant H. R. Ross British Army
Lieutenant B. Reymond RANR

Lieutenant A. L. Sargent AIF
Lieutenant W. G. Carey AIF
Sub-Lieutenant J. G. M. Riggs RNVR
Major R. N. Ingleton, Royal Marines, SEAC Representative
Warrant Officer J. Willersdorf AIF
Warrant Officer A. Warren AIF
Sergeant D. P. Gooley AIF
Sergeant C. B. Cameron AIF
Able Seaman W. G. Falls DSM RAN
Able Seaman F. W. Marsh RAN mentioned in dispatches
Able Seaman A. W. Huston DSM RAN
Corporal A. S. R. Campbell AIF
Corporal C. M. Stewart AIF
Corporal C. M. Craft AIF
Corporal R. B. Fletcher AIF
Lance Corporal J. T. Hardy AIF
Private D. R. Warne AIF
Lance Corporal H. J. Page AIF

A Note on HMAS Krait

Earliest records of the 'Krait' go back to the 1920s when she was a Japanese fishing boat named the 'Kofuku Maru' operating out of Singapore and on 6th December 1941, the day before the Japanese attack on Pearl Harbor, she left Singapore towing four barges and ostensibly bound for Japan. She was intercepted on 11th December 1941 by HMAS Goulburn, boarded, and returned to Keppel Harbour, Singapore. The crew were sent to prisoner-of-war camps in India and Ceylon.

The 'Kofuku Maru' was then used to carry refugees from Singapore to Sumatra and despite her small size, she transported some 1,300 people during the few weeks before the fall of Singapore and then she was sailed to Bombay with a load of Chinese refugees. Mr. W. R. Reynolds, a sixty-year-old Australian who had served in destroyers in the First World War, had commanded her from the outset and was later to hand her over to Services Reconnaissance Department by whom she was used in the raid on Singapore codenamed 'Jaywick' during which she was in command of Lieutenant H. E. Carse RANVR.

The 'Kofuku Maru' was renamed 'Krait' by the Royal Navy and operated under that name after she reached Bombay and was later transshipped to Australia. After the Jaywick raid she was sailed to Darwin by Lieutenant Carse and there handed over first to Captain J. Chipper AIF who was in charge of the Lugger Maintenance Section base twelve miles west of Darwin. This was another cover name used by Services Reconnaissance Department and it was in Darwin that the command of Krait passed to Lieutenant H. Williams RANVR. The Krait was used operationally from Darwin until commanded by Lieutenant Williams she sailed from Darwin to Morotai but she is remembered in the Timor Sea for her name was given to a small bay on Browse Island west of Cape Londonderry in the northern Kimberleys – an island which had been used occasionally by Services Reconnaissance Department.

After the surrender of the Japanese, Lieutenant Williams took the Krait on operations to Ambon on the island of Seram, to the Aroe Islands and finally to Labuan in Borneo where she was paid off on 12th February 1945. Thereafter she was used by the British Borneo Civil Administration and then sold for use as a timber tug during which period she was not well looked after and her condition deteriorated badly.

However, she had not been forgotten in Australia and in 1963 a Krait fund was started through the combined efforts of the Z Special Unit Association, the Lord Mayor of Sydney, Alderman H. Jenson, and the *Sun* newspaper. The Officer Commanding the Volunteer Coastal Patrol based in Sydney, Captain Harold Knobbs, was instrumental in getting the Krait, as deck cargo on the freighter Nellore, to Brisbane where many people, both civilian and from the forces, willingly gave their time working long hours to make her sufficiently seaworthy to get her to Sydney for a triumphal entry on Anzac Day 1964. Three of her crew, Lieutenant Carse, Leading Telegraphist H. Young and Able Seaman J. Jones were aboard as the only survivors of the original Operation Jaywick.

After her many thousands of miles of sea duty the Krait's work is not yet done for she lies at the headquarters of the Volunteer Coastal Patrol at The Spit in Sydney Harbour where, as a floating war memorial, she is used for sea rescue training and it is fitting that her last operational captain, the late Lieutenant H. Williams RANVR, lived not far from where she is berthed.

Appendix 2

Colombo Parties

Bungus Bay (south of Padang). May 1942
1st Lieutenant H. A. Wijnmalen put in by submarine K.15. No results. After the war it was found that Wijnmalen was taken prisoner by the Japanese, tortured and executed.

Trumon (West coast of Sumatra). December 1942. By submarine 024 Major Pel, Captain Scheepens, Lieutenant Baron S. J. van Truyll van Seroskerke (Royal Army) R. F. de Bruine (KNIL) C. Sisselar (Army) Sergeants Bosters, Hakkenburg, de Koning, Visser, Corporals van Hattem and Brynsters (Royal Marines) No results.

Lho Seumawe (East coast of Sumatra). April 1943. By submarine 024. Captain Scheepens, Lieutenants W. H. van Eek (KL) J. de Roo (KNIL) H. P. Witkamp (KNIL) Sergeants Hakkenberg, Dogers, de Leeuw and Leprandt (KM) Corporals van Hattem and Hanauer.
Result. Some information about the population.

Trumon and Meulabeuh (West coast of Sumatra). 17th and 19th April 1943. By submarine. Captain Scheepens, Lieutenants Jhr. M. W. C. de Jonge (KL) and de Roo, Sergeants Hakkenberg, Dogers, Serraris, Quinten, de Leeuw, Visser. Corporals van Hatten, British Officers – Captain Hembrey and Lieutenant Britten.
Result. Some information about the population.

North West Sumatra by British Submarine 30th April – 5th May 1944. Reconnaissance group of 2 English Officers (Captains Lowe and Arians) and 4 British Indian soldiers.

Insertion unit of Captain Scheepens, Lieutenant Sisselar, Sergeants Hakkenberg, de Lieuw, Visser, Rowing Unit of Sergeant Quinten, Corporal Hanauer and Javanese soldier Private Moerdjono. Reconnaissance group fell into hands of enemy. No results.

East Coast Sumatra by British submarine Torbay: April – May 1945. Corporal Buynster and 4 Chinese agents. Insertion unit Lieutenant de Jonge. Group returned without landing. No results.

Steel, July 1945. Landing by submarine near Soengai Tengah (west of Bagan si Api Api) in charge of British Major Lodge. No results.

Central Sumatra near Ratau Prapat. Parachute landing July 1945. Lieutenant Sisselar. No results.

Sweep, July 1945. Parachute landing near Sigli (north coast of Atjeh) in charge of Warrant Officer Lefrandt. No results.

Near Medan, 16th August 1945. Parachute landing by Naval Lieutenant Brondgeest, Ensign Classens, Corporal Bruynsters, 2 Agents. No results known.

NB. KNIL = Royal Dutch Indian Army. KL = Royal Army. KM = Royal Marine.

Appendix 3

Information about groups delivered by NEFIS

JAVA

Codename MACKEREL
Captain G. G. M. van Areken (AIF) and 2 men. Landed by Dutch submarine K12 in Radjek Winbay. 14th September 1942. Taken aboard 15th September 1942. No results.

Codename TIGER I
Naval Lieutenant W. Bergsma and 2 men. Landed in Prigi Bay, south of Madioen, by Dutch submarine on 30th November 1942.
The whole party taken prisoner and probably shot.

TIGER II
Naval Lieutenant B. Brox and 2 men. Travelled with Tiger I, 27th November 1942. Went ashore Serang Bay south coast of Java. Fell into enemy hands.

TIGER III
A Sergeant – naval – cadet Lapod from Java. Landed in Tapan Bay, south east coast of Java on 9th February 1943. No news after landing.

TIGER IV
Corporal Raden Mas Soejitno. Landed in Pang-Pang Bay, east coast of Java, south of Bali on 3rd May 1943. No further news.

TIGER V
Seaman 2nd Class Oentoeng (radio operator) landed in Pang-Pang Bay 4th May 1943. Oentoeng initially belonged

to Tiger II and would have followed the other two with the radio but remained on board when the pre-arranged signal for 'all clear' had not been given from the coast. Probably fell into enemy hands.

TIGER VI
Corporal Srinojo Papilaja.
Landed in Pang-Pang Bay 21st August 1943. Taken prisoner.

POPPY
Sergeant P. F. Reyntjes and radio operator left Australia by submarine 24th February 1945. No landing due to bad weather. Back in Australia 15th March 1945.

PARSNIP
Lieutenant Abimanjo and two radiomen. Landed in submarine in Pang-Pang area 6th June. Taken aboard 7th June. Successful.

POTATO
Sergeant H. Brouwer and 2 NCOs, 1 Indonesian. Landed from submarine at Kemirian 7th May 1945. Nothing further heard until Sergeant Brouwer arrived in Balikpapan with Hadji Talib in September 1945. He reported that the other NCO had been handed over to the Japanese.

GOLDFISH I
Lieutenant de Haas and 8 men (Indonesian). Reached the Great Paternoster Islands north of Sumbawa by submarine. Afterwards travelled by prahu to East Java (Panaroekan) where de Haas and one man landed, the rest of the party continued to the other islands. De Haas and one man caught and killed. The rest of the party returned to Australia at the end of January 1945. They obtained general and military information about Java, Lombok, Sumbawa, Flores, Celebes and the Satengah Islands.

GOLDFISH II
Sergeant L. Tahapary and 3 men (Indonesian) landed on Satengah Islands 7th June 1945, visited East Java and

several islands, did not manage to make contact with Goldfish I (one of their tasks). Evacuated to Makassar 21st November 1945. Obtained a great deal of general and military information about Madura, Java, Bali, Lombok and Makassar.

BORNEO
Apple

First Lieutenant O. L. Dryber KNIL and 2 NCOs and 5 others. The party was landed by submarine south of the mouth of the Kali Tanah Koening and operated in the area of the north-east coast of Borneo and environs south of Tarakan. Departed from Borneo 26th January 1945. Obtained information about Tarakan and north-east Borneo.

CELEBES
Lion

Party consisted of Reserve 1st Lieutenant of Engineers R. Th. Hees and 2 men. Left Darwin by prahu on 24th June 1942 for operations in Central Celebes.

Nothing further heard until evidence that some of the soldiers belonging to this party (probably joined later) were beheaded at Makassar.

Apricot

Sergeant Manopo and 4 men landed by submarine in Celebes 5th January 1945. Commander taken prisoner, the others reached Australia on 31st January 1945. Obtained some information.

NEW GUINEA
Whiting

Naval Cadet H. M. Staverman and 4 men. Operation in area Hollandia and surroundings. The whole party was killed or imprisoned. Before that some information about the locality had been passed on by radio.

OAKTREE and CRAYFISH parties: see previous text.
Trout I

Cadet Sergeant T. Tol and 8 men. Left from Mappipost

on Begul River by boat on 29th September 1943. Returned to Mappipost 30th October 1944. Obtained much
information about the locality.

Trout II

2nd Lieutenant T. Tol and 7 men. Examined south-west
coast of New Guinea by boat from 12th February 1943 to
26th May 1943, when they arrived by boat after gaining
much information.

Shark

Lieutenant T. H. Swart and 17 others and native carriers
flew by Catalina to Idenburg River (camp Bernhard) from
Merauke to collect information about Hollandia. On 25th
May 1944 they were evacuated to Hollandia.

Carrot

Lieutenant R. F. de Bruine and 16 men and native carriers
went with Shark to collect information about Wakde and
returned with Shark.

Radish

Naval Lieutenant A. Razak and 7 men landed on Kebar
plateau by parachute (this was in the Birdshead Peninsula) on 12th August 1944. Made contact with guerrilla
group of Sergeant M. C. Kokkelink. Returned to Australia with the wounded from the guerrilla group 22nd
September 1944.

Asparagus

Sergeant H. P. Swart (naval cadet in reserve) and 9 men
reached Tanah Merah on patrol for fact find on 18th July
1943 and returned 28th October 1943.

THE ARU ISLANDS

Walnut I

Major Sheldon (AMF) went ashore with 2 men from a
submarine on the Aru Islands on 15th February 1943. No
radio contact after 8th March 1943. Party fell into enemy
hands on 12th August 1943.

Walnut II
Lieutenant N. P. Monsted (AMF) and 9 men (1 Dutch-man, 2 Australians, 5 Indonesians and 1 British Indian) arrived at Aru Island by boat. After 25th July 1943 nothing further was heard of them.

CERAM
Flounder
Naval Lieutenant H. P. Hygh and 7 men. Landed from a submarine on Ceram 30th December 1942. Nothing further heard. Party taken prisoner and beheaded at Ambon.

Firtree
Lieutenant J. Tahya and 9 men. Landed at Medio in 1944. Gathered much information about the Soela Islands and Ambon.

MAJOEI ISLANDS (between Celebes and Halmahera)
Pine Needle
Sergeant Major T. M. de Bruyn and 4 men. Left Darwin by submarine on 10th September 1944. Landed on Majoei Islands and were attacked by crew of Japanese submarine on 18th April 1945. Beat off attack without any loss of life. Evacuated by Catalina on 20th April 1945. Passed on weather reports and information about ship and aeroplane movements. Obtained much information about Sangi Islands and Halmahera.

DAMAR ISLANDS (between Timor and Tanimbar Islands)
Turnip I
Sergeant Pejoh and 1 man (Tehurupun). Landed by Catalina on 26th March in Boerner Bay. Operation area Nila Island. Sergeant Pejoh drowned. Tehurupun was evacuated on 5th April 1944. Brought out information about Dobo, Ceram, Ambon.

Turnip II
Warrant Officer H. G. P. van Haren and 8 men operated

around Nila Island. They were landed from submarine 31st July 1944 and returned 21st August 1945. They obtained much information about the Ceram group and the Sermata Islands.

Salmon I

The intention of Salmon parties was to establish a line of communication from Darwin to Java by establishing bases on the intervening islands. While the plan was being executed, it was cancelled at GHQ on 19th July 1945. Prior to the establishment party a raiding party (Lieutenant N. Aaren; Lieutenant Bartelings and ten men) had gone into Damar on 12th June 1945. Salmon I flew to Damar on 14th June 1945 and were brought out on 21st August 1945 by which time the base had been established and information passed on.

Index